AF528982

Cash Me If You Can:

A Teen's Guide to Financial Freedom

Dominic Ajith Singh

Qurate
quratebooks.com

Cash Me If You Can: A Teen's Guide To Financial Freedom
Dominic Ajith Singh

© Dominic Ajith Singh

Published in 2025

© Published by

Qurate Books Pvt. Ltd.
Goa 403523, India
www.quratebooks.com
Tel: 1800-210-6527, Email: info@quratebooks.com

All rights reserved
No part of this publication may be reproduced, stored in a retrieval system, or transmitted in any form or by any means, electronic, mechanical, photocopying, recording or otherwise, without the prior permission of the author.

ISBN: 978-93-58988-03-1

Meet the Mind Behind "Cash Me If You Can: A Teen's Guide to Financial Freedom"

Hey there! I'm Dominic—your friendly guide to crushing money myths and unlocking financial freedom. With over 20 years of hustling in education, business, and career coaching, I've seen firsthand how money (or the lack of it) can make or break dreams. And let's be real—nobody taught me the money rules either. I learned them the hard way (RIP, all those vanished Christmas cash gifts!).

But here's the good news: You don't have to repeat my mistakes.

As an Educational Consultant and Career Coach, I've spent decades helping students and professionals bridge the gap between ambition and reality. But here's what kept bugging me: Why do we wait until adulthood to teach kids about money? By then, they're already drowning in credit card debt, student loans, and impulse buys (thanks, peer pressure!). That's why I wrote **Cash Me If You Can**—a no-BS, fun, and actually useful guide to money for teens. No jargon, no snooze-fest lectures—just real talk about making, managing, and multiplying your cash.

Why Trust Me?

- ✓ **Been There, Broke That:** I've made every money mistake so you don't have to.
- ✓ **Career Whisperer:** 20+ years of coaching students and professionals on turning skills into success.
- ✓ **Author Extraordinaire:** Wrote a book on bariatric surgery (random, right?)—proving I can make any topic relatable.
- ✓ **Teen-Tested:** My advice isn't from a dusty textbook—it's what today's teens *actually* need to thrive.

Fun Facts About Me:

- My first "investment" was a pack of Pokémon cards (spoiler: not a get-rich-quick scheme).
- I've survived both corporate chaos and teenage drama—making me uniquely qualified to talk money and life.
- I believe financial literacy isn't about pinching pennies—it's about designing the life you want.

Join Me On This Journey!
Whether you're a teen, parent, or educator, let's ditch the financial fear and start building confidence—one smart money move at a time. Because let's face it: The coolest thing you can be is debt-free.

Ready to level up? Grab your copy of **Cash Me If You Can**—and let's get rich (in knowledge first, cash later).

P.S. If you've ever felt clueless about cash, you're in the right place. Welcome to the no-shame zone!

☆☆☆

Introduction

Hey there, my friend! I'm so excited about the opportunity to finally talk to you about **Cash Me If You Can.** You know I've been trying to write this book for ages, but somehow, I just wasn't able to get around to it. Oh well, you know what they say; there's a time for everything. Anyway, I'm really glad to be doing this. Now you may wonder why a guy like me, with salt and pepper hair, is keen to reach out to you, especially you, a teenager. Ah well, plenty of reasons!

There are kids I know who told me that they simply didn't know how to handle money properly. I've been doing my best to guide them to be smarter with their money. But it's worrisome that in many cases, this skill isn't taught to children either at school or at home. Sadly, even I was not taught anything about financial literacy and freedom, you know?

Nobody taught me how to save money, or invest it, how to avoid getting into debt traps – nothing. Nada. Zilch. Don't even remind me of the foolish mistakes I made with the money I got from my aunts and uncles at Christmas, and Easter, and so on.

It was easy come, easy go. In fact, easier go! I could never figure out how my money could disappear that quickly. It was only much later, when I graduated, started working, and got my monthly paycheck, that I began to understand the importance of being savvy with money and I truly wished I had been that knowledgeable back in my high school or college days. But hey --- it's never too late to learn, right?

I'd like to reveal a shocking fact:

Did you know that the results from the Program for International Student Assessment (PISA) show that one in five U.S. teenage students (22 percent) lacks basic financial literacy skills?

Resource *https://www.nefe.org/news/nefe-digest/2017/can-america-compete.aspx)*

Also, teens in the U.S. (aged 18-20) have unpaid debt that has been sent to third-party collection agencies?

Do I see your jaw dropping?

Well, no surprise there, mine did too, when I read this for the first time.

Isn't it just sad and pathetic that it has come to this?

The debt includes student loans, medical expenses, and credit card loans; some have unpaid auto loans too. If only somebody had taken the trouble to educate these teens on how they can manage their money and debt, they might not be in such a colossal mess right now.

Believe me, I know how they get into this trap; I'm guessing that quite a few of you have also fallen into it, or could potentially end up there. And how do I know this? That's because I've been there myself. You know, desperately wanting to be 'in' with the cool kids; trying to wear the same outfits they wore, the same shoes, and whatnot. This list is endless. The problem is, we end up in deep trouble when we keep buying stuff that we don't need; it's something we want, just to keep up appearances, as status symbols.

Here's a pop quiz for you: What is the minimum credit card rate as of now? Any guesses?

Come on, just throw some numbers in there.

I'll tell you the answer in a bit.

But hey, no cheating!

We're not going to ask Google for the answer.

I can give you a hint, though it could be a dead giveaway.

Hmm, should I or should I not?

Alright, don't fret guys… here comes the hint: **<u>It's around your age.</u>**

Shocked again? I'm afraid it's true, though. Credit card rates start around 19%, and they're going higher each day. (Psst! Did you know that the credit card interest rates in India start from 45%?)

Wow. 19% and climbing; just like many of you, I too had no clue that not paying off credit card dues in full would have such a domino effect. When you pay just the minimum required, you end up paying heavy interest on the unpaid balance, and your credit score is affected too. You also tend to get into a vicious cycle of buying stuff on EMIs and paying more interest. But hey, don't get me wrong! I am not here to tell you that you shouldn't use credit cards – not at all. I'm going to guide you about using them right and being smart with credit cards.

On the other hand, there are plenty of examples of successful teenagers: *Jeff Bezos, Oprah, Mark Zuckerberg, Elon Musk, and Richard Branson,* to name a few; they all started working towards their dreams when they were still teenagers. Either by doing odd jobs, writing computer programs, making video games, or starting their first business.

However, you've got to remember that these guys were probably born with some smart money instincts, or were plain lucky, OR, someone taught them the ropes of saving money. Anyhow, the reason is not as important as the takeaway here: a teen can be not just financially independent, but financially successful too. Yes, it takes discipline and a little bit of work, but it is doable. You can do it, your friends can do it, your entire class can do it. And I am going to help you do it.

What is financial literacy? Well, it's simply knowing the right way to handle, budget, save, and invest money—and you must know how to do it. The decisions you make about your money today can have an impact on your future.

Fortunately, there are plenty of worksheets available that will help you in this journey of financial literacy, and I promise to either give them to you here or tell you where exactly you can get them, along with the benefits you'll receive. In fact, I'll throw in some fun but educational quizzes, and along with the printable worksheets, they will help you get better at financial literacy. So, while there are several books out there that talk about financial literacy, this book stands out as unique, all thanks to the worksheets or tasks at the end of each chapter. That's right – it's not just about giving you information; I aim ensure that you learn something.

'Cash Me if You Can' will also cover topics that you are unlikely to find in other books on financial literacy. Things like 3 Ms—Making, Managing, and Multiplying Money; modern budgeting techniques and digital tools, Peer Pressure and Impulse Buying, credit scores (what affects them, how they affect your prospects of getting loans and credit cards), and so on—all are essential parts of financial literacy. I'm sure you have a lot of questions in your mind about money, and I aim to help you find answers to those questions through this book.

So you see, this is not just another book on financial literacy; it's a practical guide that will truly empower you and make you financially independent. You've just got to put your mind to it, and I will walk with you on this exciting journey to financial freedom. It is not impossible at all. Together, we can break the shackles of debt and not having enough cash, and lead fulfilling lives. Read on to uncover the simple secrets to financial independence—and welcome to a journey that could improve your financial future!

★★★

Contents

Introduction 5

Part 1: Money Bootcamp

Chapter 1: Level Up! Why Money Matters 15

Chapter 2: Your Money Mission Control 28

Chapter 3: Banking Basics: Your Money Vault 41

Part 2: Quest for Cash: Earning and Saving

Chapter 4: From Chores to Cha-Ching: Earning Strategies 61

Chapter 5: Saving Secrets of the Super Teen 72

Part 3: Financial Fitness: Making Smart Choices

Chapter 6: Debt Decoder:
Friend or Foe? 85

Chapter 7: Protecting Your Future 100

Part 4: Long-term Financial Success

Chapter 8: Combating Peer Pressure
and Impulse Buying 119

Chapter 9: Taking Control of Your Financial Future
with Passive Income 131

Chapter 10: The Power of Philanthropy 142

Part 1

Money Bootcamp

Why are we doing this?

Bootcamp! Sounds like serious business, right? Well, it is. After all, money is absolutely important in life. It's all very well to say that money doesn't buy happiness, but hey, doesn't an ice cream, a movie, a good book, a concert, or a trip to the mall make you happy? All of those things cost money, don't they?

So, in this bootcamp, we're going to talk about what financial literacy is, why you need to master it, and all the surprisingly easy and exciting ways you can manage your money, make more money, and manage that well. We often confuse wants with needs – and when we don't have someone to show us the difference, that can have a domino effect and create huge problems. This is why, learning to set financial goals is going to be a part of this bootcamp, which, by the way, I'm sure you'll enjoy!

Knowing how to manage your bank accounts, debit/credit cards, learning to make budgets and sticking to it; learning the ropes of digital tools to not only keep your money safe but to manage it like an expert: all of this is what we are going to cover in this bootcamp. Sounds good, right? Well, I for one, can't wait to get started on this exciting journey, what about you? All set? Cool, let's dive in!

★★★

Chapter 1

Level Up! Why Money Matters

Here's a shocking fact for you:

- 751 students were part of a 2015AICPA Study.
- 57% believed they managed money well—but their actual spending habits conveyed the opposite!
- 38% had borrowed money from friends and family.
- 39%made a budget.
- 50% had less than $100 in their bank accounts at some point in the previous year.

Sadly, not much has improved over the past few years. A January 2024 EBSCO study, discovered that nearly:

- **40% of the students STILL lack basic financial literacy and money management skills.**
- **85% of the students expected that repaying the loans they had taken for their college education was going to cause them financial hardship.**

This is alarming, and very sad.

Here, we will start with the first step towards financial success, by learning what the basic financial skills are, why are they important, and what happens when you don't have financial literacy.

Introduction to Financial Literacy

I'm sure you've heard this term before you picked up this book. After all, it is discussed a lot; you are likely to have read something on the internet, or somewhere in school or college, without really being explained what it actually is. So, what exactly is financial literacy? Let's take a look:

Financial literacy means understanding essential money skills, and using them to manage your finances wisely. This includes, but isn't limited to, managing personal finances, creating budgets and making investments. When we say the words "financial literacy", we mean understanding a number of essential financial concepts and skills.

With financial literacy, you can develop a savvy and exciting relationship with money! **Financial literacy is the foundation of financial success;** after all, education is key. When you're financially literate, it becomes difficult for others to **scam** your money and wealth. Not only that, you will build a strong base that will allow you to track your spending, manage your debt well, save for your higher education, start and run a business, and even plan for your early retirement. The last one is critical! If you want to have a great retired life with no worries, and one where you travel where you want and have enough to pay your medical bills, you have to start NOW.

So how DO you become financially literate? You can listen to podcasts, subscribe to financial management blogs, and explore a wide range of books about financial literacy.

OR

You can diligently follow **'Cash Me If You Can'**, which is thorough and covers everything to make you smart with money. Like I told you earlier, you're not going to be a passive reader here. I will make sure that you participate, through worksheets, and a few fun quizzes.

Do you know why financial literacy is more important now than ever? Well, earlier, the only way to purchase any product – from an appliance to an apartment – was by paying money that you actually had; either cash or cheque. But I'm sure you are aware that this is not the case today. Everything is available on credit, and that can create problems, as it induces people to buy things they can't really afford.

Now, if you want to know the pitfalls of not being financially literate, we can look at a real-life example. I'm sure you've heard of celebrities like sports stars and actors who seem to be rolling in money, and then, one fine day you hear that they've been arrested or have cases piled up against them in court.

Here is one such example:

I'm sure you have heard of Nicolas Cage; if you haven't, just Google him, and you'll see that at one time, he was one of Hollywood's top actors, earning millions. His acting skills earned him roles in some of the highest-grossing movies of his time, catapulting him into stardom and riches. But guess what? He managed his money poorly and came crashing down to Earth in 2009. He owed back taxes worth million of dollars! What caused his downfall? Bizarre purchases like a dinosaur skull, lavish residences across the world, and whatnot. These were unproductive purchases. He put his money into things that didn't give him anything back. The reason – he was NOT financially literate!

Of course, coming into a lot of money suddenly often tends to make people egoistic and brash, and they end up becoming bankrupt and, in some cases, fugitives from the law. I still can't help thinking that had Nicolas Cage been truly financially literate, he wouldn't have made those mistakes. I hope that this unfortunate example has succeeded in conveying why it's necessary to have financial literacy.

Being financially literate can not only help you remain debt-free or have minimal debt, but it will also prepare you to pay for financial emergencies, stop you from making bad financial choices, and help you turn your dreams into reality. To top it all, financial literacy will make you more confident, and capable of making major life decisions properly.

We will now move on to how money management can impact your personal freedom and opportunities, and how you can enjoy long-term benefits like wealth creation and a happy, secure, early retirement.

Importance of Money Management

Helmets and shoulder pads worn by football players have an important job: they protect the players from serious injury, a distinct possibility in a contact sport. Think of money in the same way; it protects you from the uncertainties of life. Of course, money also provides things that are essential for living, like food and shelter. That's why, it is necessary to manage it well.

Like they say, "no pain, no gain." Now what could this possibly mean in our context of money management? Well, it's just that we can't have it all. At least, not right away. We are going to have to be disciplined and make a few sacrifices early on in life so that later in life, we can be comfortable. This means tightening your belt and learning to say 'No' to yourself and friends when you know that it's not strictly necessary to spend, or when it's not possible.

Not everyone is likely to be in the same state financially. You may very well have friends who seem to have plenty of money, and they may want you to join them in expensive pursuits. Don't I know it! I've been through it, after all. Peer pressure is real. It can be stifling. But you have to learn to resist the temptation. Now, I don't at all mean to say that you should never have any fun in your early years, and the only thing you should do is spend on strictly necessary stuff. Not at all! Fun is necessary too; it's just the amount you spend on it that you need to watch.

If you've seen the sitcom 'Two Broke Girls', you would have seen how a rich girl, Caroline, suddenly goes broke because her dad was running a Ponzi scheme and finally got caught. She had to make drastic lifestyle changes as her money was all frozen or seized. Now, this is way, way, harder to do, than to be a little conservative with your money at first and go on to make money later in life. Coming down from a lavish lifestyle is extremely difficult.

When you are financially disciplined in your teens and youth, you can certainly have a much more comfortable life later on. Investing money in the right instruments at the right time can help you multiply your money so that you accumulate wealth. You can have an independent and enjoyable early retirement, without having to depend on the mercy of the state or your family. Doesn't that sound good?

Putting your money to work for you is what you need to do; of course, here, we are going to discuss how exactly you can do it. Getting a good education is an investment. It opens more doors for your career and a better job. Even if your dream is to start your own business, getting a management degree will help you tremendously, no doubt.

Quick question: Do you know how many students take a loan to go to college?

Take a wild guess – you've nothing to lose.

Well, it's as high as **60%** and the national student **debt is 1.77 trillion US dollars!** The most critical issues for students, the study found, were:

- Insecurity over housing and food.
- Poor understanding of credit.
- Losing money on investments because of uninformed choices.
- Credit card debt.

All these factors cause high stress to students, making it difficult for them to focus on academics. Some are lucky to have wise parents or rich aunts or uncles who create a college fund for them, but the rest have to make it on their own. So, if you're among the latter, start planning while you're still in high school. Say no to a few luxuries now so that you are not burdened later.

Opportunities with Money Management

As a student, when you learn to manage your money, the first benefit is that you understand its true value. Knowing how to budget, save, and invest your money will be the guiding force for you in making savvy financial decisions later in life.

It goes without saying that money management means a lot of careful planning and sound decision-making – these are critical skills you will develop over time when you learn money management.

If you look at the latest methods of investment like digital assets and crypto currency, they are created using algorithms and math concepts. This means, an opportunity for you to develop your tech skills as well.

When more teens become financially stable and independent, it helps to bring down inequality and poverty in society, which benefits the country. Money management teaches you to make good choices regarding financial products, and what's more, you will be well-prepared for real-life situations.

When teens like you become aware of money management, you develop responsible spending habits and become cautious about overspending. Your thinking will be channeled towards productive spending and investments – and that again, will help you be financially independent and successful.

Ever dreamed about hiking up Mount Kilimanjaro? Walking through the tulip gardens in Holland? Taking a cruise to the Caribbean? Want to pursue a college degree at an Ivy League school? Have a great idea for a startup and be your own boss? Well, you can achieve all of these and more when you manage your money properly. Travel the world, set up your own business, go back to school at any time (or many times), and live life to the fullest, when you manage your money right.

You don't have to necessarily wait till you're grey-haired and weak-kneed to travel and enjoy life! Being diligent in your teens can help you achieve this in early adulthood too.

Now, let's look at a couple of examples where smart money management helped teens become successful:

Ryan Hrejlac: Twenty years ago, as a six-year-old boy, Ryan was devastated when he heard from his first-grade teacher in Ontario, Canada, that children were dying in Africa due to lack of clean drinking water. At that moment he decided to do something about it. He begged his parents for help who agreed to pay him money to do extra chores. He thought that $70 would suffice to build a well, which he earned in seven months. When he realized it would take $2,000 instead, he did chores for his neighbors, and got others to pitch in, and spoke to anyone that he could. In 12 months, he raised the money needed and finally built the first well in the Angolo Primary School in Uganda. There was no stopping for this little boy after that. He persisted in his efforts; graduated with a degree in International Development and Political Science, and joined a non-profit, all while raising money for his wells.

Today the Ryan's Well Foundation provides clean drinking water to thousands of African children, saving them from death and disease; the children look upon him as a godsend. As a little child, Ryan managed the money he earned and received as donations so well, that he was able to do something for people he had never even met in life. While this is not your typical rags-to-riches story, it is worth knowing and sharing, and an amazing example of what right money management can achieve. Hey, if a six-year-old could do it, so can you!

Michael Furdyk: "Work together to create a global network for young people who either have an idea that they want to develop, or who want the opportunity to work on someone else's project" This was the foremost idea in Michael's head when he came up with his brainchild, Taking IT Global. He developed a social network to encourage teens and young adults to be part of discussions to boost global awareness and to support actions that have impacts on their local communities. He and his friends created an online technology and sold it – making him a millionaire almost overnight. Of course, he had the support of his family; but he used it productively, rather than blow the money.

He wanted to give back to society and help nurture youngsters who are talented but have no family or financial support. He strongly felt that youngsters need to be more involved in global issues, and actively encouraged and supported them by providing global education programs. Michael has received several awards from tech giants like Microsoft. He not only makes money himself but educates youth and empowers them to also do the same. Isn't that awesome?

I personally found these real-life stories highly inspiring. I bet you are impressed as well. It's clear that when an individual becomes financially literate and has excellent money management skills, it's not just that person, but the whole society, country, and even the world, that stands to benefit.

Alrighty, it's time for us to put on our thinking caps. Here's a small exercise for you. In this worksheet, list out your financial goals, both long-term and short-term. Of course, you can have as many as you like, but for now, think of the five most important goals. It's also fine if you have less than five.

1. My Financial Goals

LONG TERM GOALS	SHORT TERM GOALS

2. Make a Travel Plan

I'm sure there must be someplace you have been eager to visit. So, imagine you are going on a solo trip for 4 days. Write down the place you want to visit and make a budget for it. List the attractions you don't want to miss, and make a list of budget accommodations available. Also, note down your mode of travel and commute within your destination.

Travel tickets	
Accommodation	
Food	
Sight-seeing	
Commuting	
Shopping (souvenirs)	

3. Education Planning

Make a table to compare the courses you are interested in.

Institution/University	Course	Duration	Cost

4. Brainstorm Ideas for a Business

It can be something very simple, like a pet-sitting venture; rearranging closets, or anything you can think of.

Note down how much you think you need to spend on advertising your services/business, and ideas on how to expand.

Well, then, I hope you're all done setting your financial goals so that we can move on to the next step. Here we are going to talk about mastering the 3 M's of Money – Making, Managing, and Multiplying. Now don't look so surprised! It's totally doable. Yes, even as a student. Like I've been saying right from the beginning, it is not impossible, and you don't have to live like a monk to be financially independent or successful.

★★★

Chapter 2

Your Money Mission Control

I'd like to share a little story about a teenager—a colleague's son who missed the bus. Let's call him Nathan. Nathan had collected a substantial amount of money doing chores in the neighborhood, and he also had some of his 'Christmas money' in hand. He was all agog about the Billie Eilish concert that was a few weeks away still. She is his favorite singer and he was dying to attend the concert.

A few days before the concert, a group of his friends decided to go on a holiday to a beach resort a little away. When they asked him, Nathan said yes without thinking. He had a great time for sure, but he ended up spending quite a bit of money there. Horror of horrors, he realized he didn't have enough money left to purchase the concert ticket now! He did extra chores at home and in the neighborhood, but he still fell short. So it was Billie Eilish live on his computer – he missed out on what could have been the single most exciting event in his life. It was then that he thought, "If only I had put the ticket money aside. If only." But it was too late for that, wasn't it?

By now, most of you probably know that Mark Zuckerberg and a couple of his friends created the social networking platform called Facebook while still at Harvard. At first, it was only available to Harvard students when it was launched in 2004. After making it available to other college students, it was opened to the general public in 2006. Today, Zuckerberg is a multi-millionaire who has not only acquired WhatsApp and Instagram but also launched another social platform called Threads. He created a parent company called Meta Platforms under which all these entities exist. Consistent work, money management, and disciplined decisions helped this teenager make, manage, and multiply his money something like 100 times probably!

Alright, let's talk about how you can do the three M's yourself.

Making Money

You probably had not really known this, but you can provide for yourself, and be a part of the economy of this great country. If you earn enough, you could soon become a tax-paying citizen. Isn't that cool?

Now you don't need to start with a fancy job title or a posh workplace. You need to be practical. As a teenager, you can do part-time work. There are a lot of different types of jobs that can be done. Let's zip through the things you can do!

- Work in cafes and restaurants, part-time when you have school, and full-time during holidays and weekends.
- Do chores at home to add to your allowance and at your neighbor's for some extra cash.
- If you're already at college, there are plenty of ways for you to add to your stash right on campus.
- Those with creative abilities can really take it up a notch with gigs now and then.
- Freelance work in writing is an amazing opportunity.

- I bet you're good at making videos – you can make a bunch of dollars out of them.
- Work as an intern at a company that is in a related industry to your course.
- Online jobs – this includes taking surveys, selling stuff, game participation, and more.
- Start your own business! There are loads of teens who have started off with something very small and gone on to become—hold your breath—millionaires. I kid you not.

Now one thing I would like to say here is that you've got to balance your academics and your work. Don't get too carried away by the idea of making some big bucks that you leave your homework and assignments untouched.

You have to manage both – find that sweet spot where you're able to handle it all just fine. See, the thing is, right now, you don't have to think in terms of making a fortune immediately. Sure, you need your big dream and long-term goals and all that. But you've got to set short-term goals, and try to make the dough for them.

Say, for example, you want to buy the latest Mac—after all, it will help in your studies too. That is a long-term goal, or at best, a medium-term one. Macs are not cheap, after all. You may need to work a little more to earn extra, and cut back on some other spending. Your short-term goals could be stuff like buying a new pair of jeans, joining a gym or aerobics/Zumba class, and so on.

You will be able to do all of this, as long as you're not slacking off, either at work or at school. You need money to do all the stuff you want to, and there are ways that you can make that money.

This is the age where you're full of beans, and you've just got to put your mind to it. You definitely can. Sure, it's not easy, but it's not impossible either.

Managing Money

Okay, so we've seen the many different ways in which you can make money, and most of them are pretty straightforward. Making money is actually the easy part; managing it well is harder.

Budgeting

This is the most basic part of money management. You need to have a budget. What exactly is a budget, though? Let's have a look:

In its very simple form, a budget can be divided into three parts:

- It is nothing but just looking at the money you've got coming in.
- And then deciding how much of it you can spend.
- And then how much you need to save.

Everyone, from the richest corporations to the minimum wage earners, must have a budget.

At your age, having a monthly or even weekly or fortnightly budget, depending on when you get paid, is good enough. Knowing your income is the first thing to do; this could be your allowance from home, payments from part-time jobs or gigs, or a combination of both. When you know exactly how much you have at the beginning of each month, it's much easier to make a budget.

a. Budget Categories

To make it easy for you, the ideal thing for you to do is break your budget into two main categories: Saving and Spending.

Now under Saving, you could include these items:

- Putting money into your savings account
- College fund
- Money for investments
- Purchase of assets like a car, laptop, or similar

Then you have your Expenses or Spending:

- Essentials like food, phone bill, gas for your car, stationery
- Others like clothes, gym memberships, OTT subscriptions, entertainment, gifts, eating out, and so on.
- In case you contribute towards household expenses like groceries and utilities, include them too.

b. Budget Strategies

You can create different subheadings for your expenses and decide that you will spend a maximum of X amount of dollars on each. Let us understand this with a simple example:

- $200 on food
- $50 for phone
- $30 for OTT subscription

You get the drift, don't you? Once you make this budget, try to spend only that much for that category. But this could be hard if you're budgeting for the first time. You can start with deciding that you will spend a certain amount of money each month, and stick to it.

For example, let's say you get $500 each month. You consciously decide to save $150 each month, and only spend $350, on all the items combined.

Now in the expense category, there are two further types of expenses – the first is obviously, your needs, and the second is more of wants. Now you may argue that clothes are not wants, they are needs. Sure, they are; but what type of clothes are needs and what all are wants? Practical, comfortable, and reasonably priced clothing – those are needs. Expensive branded stuff to fit in with the cool kids – those are definitely wants!

For every type of expense, you can stop and think whether it's a need or a want. Even when it comes to food. You can either choose to have food from your college or university cafeteria (buying meal coupon blocks or monthly subscriptions), or make sandwiches at home, which is healthier and less expensive, or you can have fast food from restaurants which is much unhealthier, and much more expensive.

Another thing you need to remember is that your essential expenses or needs you can easily know how much you spend. All you have to do is check your previous month's food bills, etc. It is the non-essentials that are difficult to predict. For example, an outing to the mall with friends can easily cause you to spend more than you thought you would. It is nearly impossible to predict exactly how much these things will cost you.

Here are a few strategies:

- Saving first – you first put a certain amount of money into your savings account, as soon as you get your allowance or wages. The money that is left over, you spend in whatever way you want. Now this makes a lot of sense! If you decide to spend first, and then save what's left over, you may find that there's not much left over on the 30th of the month! And that, my friend, is something that can land you in trouble later.

- Zero-based – this method says that when your expenses are deducted from your income, the result should be zero. Once you have an estimate of each category of budget, you keep dividing your income till you touch zero, based on those estimates.
- 50/30/20 rule – this says that 50% of your available money must be used for essentials, 30% for other not-so-essential expenses, and 20% is what you should save. But feel free to put more into savings if you don't have many expenses; or if you want to save up for a big purchase in the near future, check where you can squeeze. You may have to sacrifice a little, like foregoing visits to the mall or gaming arena with friends.

Always look to save as much as you can – it will serve you well later, believe me! If it's not possible for you to cut existing costs but want to save more, see if it will be possible for you to take up a part-time job or some gigs – a side hustle depending on your talents, that will pay you more.

c. Make Adjustments

Now I know that when you make a budget for the first time, it may not always work as we're discussing here. It's super easy to say what must be done, but the reality could be very different. Let's assume that you are overshooting a category – say food. If so, adjust your budget, and reduce spending elsewhere to accommodate food costs. Or let's say you are spending much less than you expected; well then, put it quickly towards your college fund, or a car purchase, or you can always invest it.

If you're overspending on non-essential items like clothes or eating out, make a conscious effort to curb these wants and wait till you are more financially comfortable.

d. Track your Spending

Oh yeah, it's easy to say that you must make a budget and stick to it. But let me tell you, it's not a walk in the park! It can be very hard. Often, expenses creep up on you suddenly, knocking the wind out of you. Let's say you have a car – a second-hand one. It can break down suddenly, necessitating repairs that can throw your budget into a tizzy!

Plus, we're living in the digital world today – it's not just about cash anymore, is it? Things were definitely simple when you would get a wad of notes at the beginning of the month, and you had to carefully spend out of it, making it last the whole month. Now with mobile payments and gazillion cards, you never know where and how fast your money is going. Unless you track it diligently.

But the digital world has its benefits too! You can get a budgeting app, which will help you track your money, make the budget each month, and show you where exactly your money is going – and not with boring long text, but via charts. How cool is that?

The problem is that when you don't track each dollar spent, you think it's just one burger, only one pack of chips, it just costs $2 or $5, but these little purchases add up and manage to rip a hole the size of a ball field in your budget before you can see that.

According to a study by the Education Data Initiative, a college student in the US spends on food this way:

- $673 in a month on average
- $570 on a monthly campus meal plan
- $410 eating off campus
- $263 on home-cooked meals (when they also eat off campus)

They also admitted to spending:

- An average of $40-50 a month on alcohol
- Heavy drinkers – close to $100 on alcohol

When you see these numbers, doesn't it all become much clearer?

Tracking your daily spending will let you know what expenses you can cut. For example, buying coffee from a café may be eating into your budget. Why not make it at home and bring it with you in a go-to cup?

Similarly, you can often get great clothes at Goodwill for a fraction of the price you would have to pay in big stores. You can also get some clothes from stores like Target, and save a little.

e. Look For Discounts

One great way to cut your spending is to use coupons and discounts. Saving 10% on a single purchase may not seem like much, but those small savings add up by the end of the month, and you'll find you've saved a bunch of money.

f. Learn from Your Mistakes

Hey, it happens! Everyone makes mistakes; we're only human. The important thing is to LEARN from those mistakes, and avoid repeating them. If you've spent more and failed to save, sit down and think about how and why it happened. Could you have avoided that extra expense? Practice makes perfect; you need to develop the habit of responsible spending and saving effectively. Let your mistakes motivate you to do better next time.

g. Set SMART Goals

SMART stands for Specific, Measurable, Achievable, Realistic, and Time-Bound. This method is a great way to achieve your goals, financial or otherwise.

- Specific: You need clear goals, not vague ideas. The better defined your goal, the easier you can achieve it. You can divide your goals into:
    - Short-term goals (within a year):like attending a big concert or buying a laptop
    - Medium-term goals (within five years): like traveling abroad
    - Long-term goals: like buying a house, building a retirement corpus, etc.
- Measurable: You should be able to measure your goal; for example, “I want to save $6000 in two years”, or something similar. Now you have something to work towards.
- Achievable: Well, you need to be practical. Defining a goal like buy a house, car and be completely debt-free by the time you are 30 is unachievable for most. Unless you’re some mad genius with an awesome job.
- Realistic: You need to think of saving up for something meaningful that will actually improve your financial well-being. It can be slightly challenging so it pushes you to perform, but it must be realistic.
- Time-bound: This is critical. Set a date by which you must achieve a certain goal. That will definitely keep you going and help you achieve the goal as it will play with your mind.

Breaking down your goals into smaller chunks – say every week or month, can help you, in case a yearly plan overwhelms you. Baby steps are good to take. Focus on each one, and you’ll be there.

Multiplying Money

Al righty! Now that we’ve seen how we can make and manage our money, it’s time to learn how to make it grow. Just like plants need to be watered for growth, you have to nurture your money – in different ways.

As a teen and a student, you have limited money, sure; you also don't have the entire galaxy of investment options open to you – yet. But you can definitely make a start. Like we said earlier, baby steps. They will get you where you want to go, every single time. Remember: Every dollar saved, is a dollar earned. Humble beginnings often lead to mind-blowing heights. But it's important to take that first step.

Saving Money

We already saw how we can save money. From your monthly funds, set aside X dollars right at the beginning, and don't touch that money. Open a savings account in addition to your normal checking account. Not only will the money in your savings account remain safe, but you can even earn a little interest on your balance. This is the first step toward saving and investing you can take as a young adult, or even before you become an adult.

It pays to start small. As your savings account balance grows, you can use some of the money at a later point to invest it in instruments that give you more returns – more bang for your buck as they say!

Now you may think that these are big things that teens have no business doing, but that's not true. Even as teenagers, you can put your money to work by choosing the right investment avenues. We will guide you on this, and you can also talk to your parents to know where to invest.

The Power of Compounding

You need to know how powerful the impact of compounding can be. If you have 300 dollars with you and you simply keep it locked up in your cupboard, after say five years, presuming you haven't touched that money, you will still have only 300 dollars. But if you put it in a bank, you will earn interest on it and that money will grow. We will look at all this in detail a bit later.

Well, I think that's quite a bit of discussion we've had on the three M's of money. You now know how to **make** money, how to **manage** it (the most important part), and how to **multiply** it.

Before we move on, here are a couple of exercises for you:

#1. Make a list of Jobs you can do

#2. Make a Budget listing your monthly income and expenses

Income	Expenses
Allowance:	Food:
Wages:	Commute:
Freelance gigs:	Gas:
	Stationery:
	Laundry:
	Entertainment:
	Subscriptions and Memberships:

(Feel free to add more expense heads according to your lifestyle and habits)

#3. Note Down where you're overspending and think of alternatives

All done? Alrighty then, it's time to move on to the next stop on our journey to financial freedom!

☆☆☆

Chapter 3

Banking Basics: Your Money Vault

Do you have a bank account?

If not, you're not alone!

A surprising number of teens don't have their own accounts. But having a bank account is more than just a place to stash your cash; it's the foundation of your financial future. It's the base for building your financial life.

Tracking your spending and income becomes much simpler, too. But do you know the sad part?

According to a National Financial Awareness Survey by Junior Achievements USA here's the reality:

- 17% of US teenagers, that is almost one in every five, have never been to a bank
- 34% of US teens don't have their own bank account

- 35% of teens that do have an account, got them when they were 12 or younger. Which means, their parents did it for them.

This shows most teens are not bothered enough to go and open an account themselves, and if they have one, they aren't bothered about becoming bank savvy. This is really sad.

Well, I hope you're among those teens who do have an account; and if you don't, it would be a great idea to open one right away. So, are you ready to unlock the secrets of savvy banking? Let's dive in!

Understanding Bank Accounts

What exactly is a bank account?

- It is a way for you to keep your money safe, and use it when you need it.
- You open an account with a bank and deposit the money into it, and the bank keeps a record of all the money you put into it, and all that you withdraw.

Are you wondering how safe your money is in the bank, after watching bank heists in movies and TV shows?

Well, you don't have to worry. All banks are insured. This means, that even if thieves hold up the bank and take away all the cash, the bank will get it back from the insurance company.

How does having a bank account work?

The bank will issue you a debit card and/or a check book, and you can use them to buy things and withdraw cash from the bank. If you are not yet 18 years old, you will need a parent or guardian to be the co-owner of the account. You may be asked to provide any of the following documents at the time of opening the account:

- Driver's License or any Government issued photo ID
- Social Security card
- Birth certificate
- Passport
- If you are employed and are in the tax-paying bracket, the taxpayer ID card

The bank may set limits on your cash withdrawals from ATMS, spending limits (per day or month), and account alerts that notify your parent or guardian, letting them keep a track of how much you're spending.

Bank	Monthly Fee	Minimum Deposit	Parental Controls	Special Features
Capital One MONEY Teen Checking	$0	$0	Yes	No overdraft fees
Chase First Banking℠	$0	$0	Yes	Budgeting tools
Alliant Credit Union Teen Checking	$0	$0	Yes	High APY on savings

Benefits Of A Bank Account

So now, you may wonder what exactly are the benefits of opening a bank account. Here they are:

- It can help you learn basic financial skills
- You can make deposits and withdrawals yourself
- You'll become familiar with using a debit card.
- You'll learn to use online and mobile banking
- Budgeting, saving, and investing becomes easier
- Being smart about money management starts here
- It helps build your credit score

Common Pitfalls You Need To Be Wary About

Yay! Congratulations on finally deciding to open your own bank account.

But... a word of caution...

While it's exciting to have your own account and you can learn a lot from it, **there are some things you need to be aware of:**

1. *Overdrawing your account*

You may get carried away when you get your debit card and swipe away till you finish everything in your account—and then some.

Ergo, you need to know your account balance at all times so that you never overdraw your account. This will bring down your credit score, not to mention you end up paying hefty O/D fees.

2. *Sharing Account Information*

- Identity theft is a huge problem nowadays.
- People gain access to your bank accounts, credit cards, and even social security numbers, and take over your identity to empty your account.
- You need to be extremely careful to not let this happen.
- Never share your account number, card PIN, password, and so on with anyone.
- That info needs to be under wraps always.
- If you give out these details, your account becomes vulnerable and you may lose your money.
- Always keep your computer and phone locked with a strong password.

Many banks have strict policies against account holders lending their debit cards even to family members. It is only supposed to be used by you; in case something goes wrong, you may not be able to get a solution from your bank if they know that someone else was using your card or operating your online banking with your knowledge.

If you have a check book, make sure you don't sign on blank checks and keep them around.

3. *Scams and fraud*

Now there are a lot of people out there who only want to scam you.

You've got to have your wits about you whenever there's any phone call about your bank.

Some random person may call you or text you or even send you emails asking for your account details; but you should never respond to them, as no bank would ever ask for your details in this manner.

Friends may ask for your PIN, maybe when you've to quickly buy some food or drinks, they may not have bad intentions either; but it's better to be safe than sorry, so politely refuse.

Make up an excuse if you like.

4. *Not Being Aware of Fees*

Each bank may charge differently for services they provide, like overdrafts, ATM withdrawals, maintenance, and so on.

It's wise to know how much your bank charges so that you can act accordingly; for example, make sure to only use ATMs in your bank's network so that you don't pay heavy fees.

A Bank Account Matters

Think of a bank account as your personal money vault—a secure place to store and manage your hard-earned cash. It's a key tool for tracking your spending, saving for goals, and even building a good credit score.

Different Types Of Accounts

Banks offer different types of accounts, but these are the most important ones as far as you are concerned:

- ✓ Checking Accounts: This is the account from which you spend money for daily needs like buying food, paying for gas or the bus, and so on. It pays a very low rate of interest, as the bank has to ensure they keep all the money in it so that you can use it as you require.
- ✓ Savings Accounts: This is the account you use to save money for a rainy day. Build up a good sum to say, buy a car, pay for college, do some traveling, and so on. A savings account pays a better rate of interest as compared to a checking account.

How Do You Choose The Right Bank Account?

Well, that depends on a lot of things!

Obviously, you want to discuss this at home with your parents, and you want the bank to be reasonably close to you.

If a few banks are nearby, you should probably go check them out.

You don't want an account in a bank where El Groucho is the teller, right?

You want friendly, helpful staff who won't consider you a small fry and ignore you.

Here are some other things:

- Low monthly fees, ATM charges, overdraft fees, and NSF (non-sufficient funds) penalties
- Zero or very low balance requirements
- User-friendly process for depositing and withdrawing money
- Parental supervision that allows a parent or guardian to guide you to manage your account better
- Good digital experience like internet banking and mobile app

- Make sure the account is insured by the FDIC or Federal Deposit Insurance Corporation.
- You should be able to contact an actual person when you have a query or problem, and not have only automated responses or digital tools for query resolution.

Setting Up Your Bank Account

This itself is pretty straightforward. I'll list out the steps here to make it easy to follow:

- Finalize the bank you want to open an account with, after comparing fees, etc. as mentioned above.
- Get the necessary documents ready, like:
  - Address proof
  - Government-issued ID
  - Social security card
- Take a parent or guardian with you if you are not 18 yet
- Talk to the relevant bank representative in charge of account opening
- Understand all the terms and conditions including fees, limits, and balance requirements
- Fill in the necessary forms; your guardian/parent may need to co-sign your application
- Make the initial deposit. Some banks may have a minimum amount you need to deposit, while others may not. In any case, you are always free to deposit any amount over the minimum requirement.
- You will then receive detailed account information from the bank. Read it carefully and follow the instructions to set up your PIN for your debit card, phone banking, and internet banking (if available). Most banks offer online and mobile banking features that let you manage your money easily. You can check your balance, view recent transactions, transfer money between accounts, pay bills online, and even deposit checks using your phone's camera. These

features can save you both time and trips to the bank. The bank may ask for your preference for debit cards or checks. Make sure to store your checkbook in a safe place.

Using Debit Cards Safely

Shifting preferences are very evident when it comes to the method of spending money in the bank.

A debit card is like a magic wand for your money, allowing you to access your funds without carrying cash.

Some crazy but true facts:

- Only 18% use a checkbook, while a whopping 62% use debit cards.
- Annuity. Org found in a study that 32% of the teens did not know the difference between debit cards and credit cards.

How Do Debit Cards Work?

A debit card is usually issued to everyone who opens a bank account.

You can use this card to avoid carrying cash with you.

If you lose cash, it's nearly impossible to get it back.

But if you lose your card, you can simply inform the bank and get it blocked so that nobody can use it to swipe your money.

The bank will issue you a new one, and you can set a new PIN for it, just like you did for your earlier card.

You need to remember that you can only swipe your debit card for the amount you have in your account. If you continue to swipe your card beyond that, you will have to pay hefty fines.

So, it's good to be mindful of how much money you have in your account. You can also use your debit card to withdraw cash at ATMs, in case you need cash at certain places.

Debit cards can be used not just at shops you go to, but also online.

Now some of these brands' stuff is pretty steeply priced; if you're completely dependent on the allowance you get from home, I'd suggest going easy on online shopping! Yes, it is very tempting. And when you can shop with just a few taps on your phone, it is super easy too.

Well, it's how you define enjoyment that can make a difference!

Ben Franklin also said, "Beware of little expenses; a small leak will sink a great ship."

Now we come to the crux of the matter. We already talked about how we think that a dollar here or there won't really matter, but it does! And when you swipe your card repeatedly, you may end up spending money that you don't actually have yet.

So you see, that little detail that you may have groaned at – parental controls on your account – may actually help.

"Needs vs. Wants" Quiz

Scenario: You have $50. You need new sneakers for gym class ($40), but you also really want that new video game ($50). What do you do?

A) Buy the video game now and worry about sneakers later.

B) Buy the sneakers now and save up for the video game.

C) Ask your parents for more money.

Answer: B) is the best choice. Prioritizing needs over wants is essential for smart money management.

Your bank is likely to place limits on the number of withdrawals you can make in a month, the amount you can pay by card in a day, and so on. When your bank issues you a card, they will also give you a flyer or manual that has all this information in detail. Make sure you read it properly and understand everything before you just toss it into the trash can.

Budgeting and Digital Tools

Budgeting doesn't have to be a chore. Digital tools can make it a breeze!

Here is some information that should set you thinking.

A study conducted by Annuity. org says that while 86% of the students wanted to invest, 45% did not do so, because they were not confident.

So, what can you do to avoid or at least significantly reduce stress related to money matters?

Effective Budgeting Tips

Well, one of the most important things you can do is create proper budgets. There are many ways of doing this. Let's take a look.

- Use a diary and manually write down your income and expected expenses.
- Use spreadsheets on your computer, which are more organized.
- Download budgeting or money management apps on your mobile.

We have already discussed how to make a budget in a previous chapter, but there's something I would like to add here.

Now that you have a bank account, set up an automatic transfer from your checking account to your savings or other account, where a fixed sum is deposited each month. This will be forced saving for you, which is good! This money will grow steadily over time. Now using manual methods can be very messy for teens.

A digital tool, on the other hand, is likely to be much more comfortable and easier for you to use.

Before we explore different tools, it's important to know the safety measures you must take while using them. After all, you will enter information about your bank account, cards, and some personal details too.

- Scan the privacy statement and verify that they will not share your financial info with third parties. If they have no privacy statement, avoid the app.
- Check if the app uses 128- or 256-bit encryption, and a two-factor authentication process to ensure security.

- It makes sense to use apps that are released by reputed institutions with expertise in the secure processing of user information.
- Only download apps from official app stores so that you don't invite spyware and viruses.
- Read reviews left by users and shortlist the ones with the highest ratings.
- Install antivirus on your computer and mobile devices, and set strong passwords on them too.
- Avoid using your financial app while you are using free Wi-Fi hotspots in public spaces. If you need to access your info while you're not at home, it's best to stick to mobile data, or at least use a VPN to encrypt the connection.

Mobile Apps That Help with Budgeting and Money Management

Now that you're aware of how to be safe when using apps, let us check out some of the best mobile apps that help you manage your money properly.

1. **Money Manager Expense & Budget** (Apple Rating: 4.8)

This app from Real byte Inc. is a personal account management app that simplifies expense tracking, budgeting, and so on. You can change the default settings on the basis of your requirements as the functions are highly customizable. It has some awesome features like:

- Easy to enter data wherever and whenever you want
- See your expenses in a graph, including fluctuations
- Enter data and view stats
- Has search and calculator functions
- You can set categories and sub-categories as you want
- Use multiple currencies

- Manage your debit & credit cards, and all your accounts at the same time
- Plan weekly, monthly, or yearly budgets with the budget planning feature
- Use the calendar view and change the month start date
- Check stats by week, month, or year
- Set up automated money transfers between your accounts
- Sort expenses by recipient and view them in graphical form
- Backup and restore your data via iCloud, iTunes, and email.
- Create payment profiles to easily enter regular expenses – say cafeteria, gas, etc.

Here are some of the screens from the app:

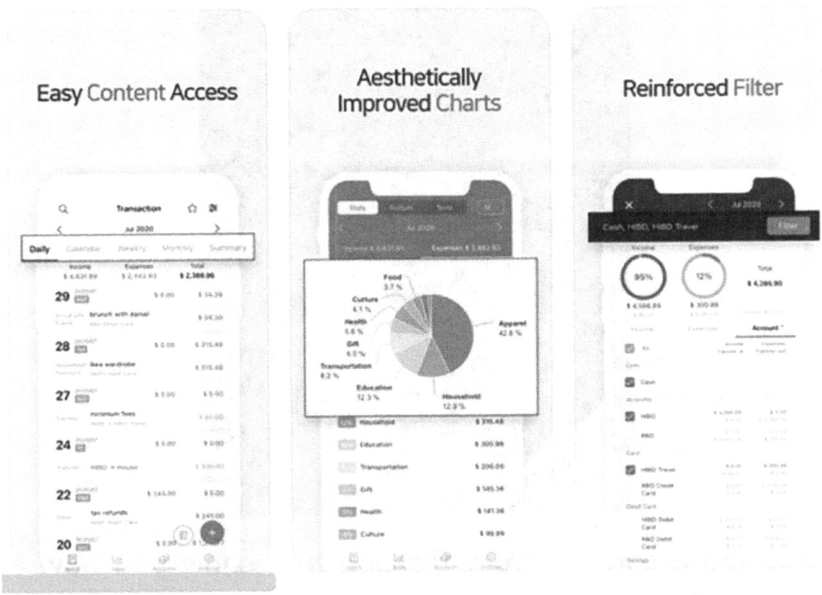

2. Pocket Guard – Android and iOS

It has a rating of 4.4 on Google Play and 4.6 on App Store.

It's super easy to use, and the best part is that it points out places where you can save your money.

It analyzes your expenditure and makes recommendations. It also categorizes your expenses automatically. However, in the free version, you don't have many options for customization. To use the more advanced features, you need to pay a monthly subscription.

Adding a bank Account:

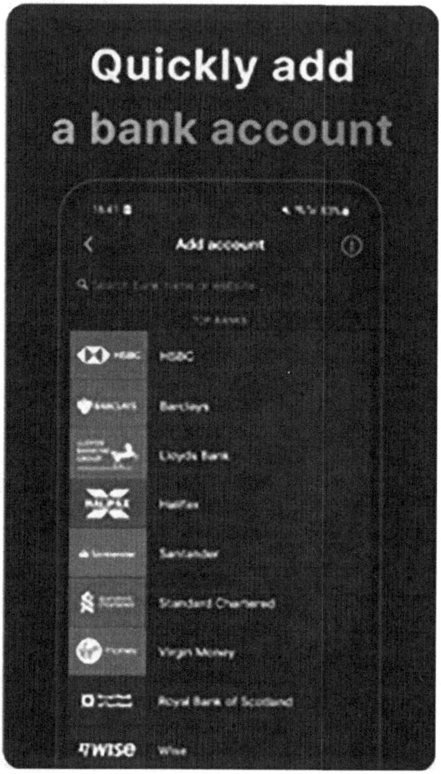

Some more screens from the app that show you how to budget, view analytics, and cash flows:

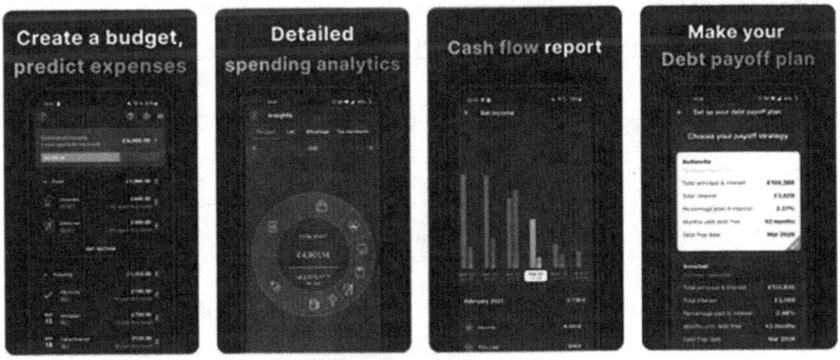

Your Bills are organized like this:

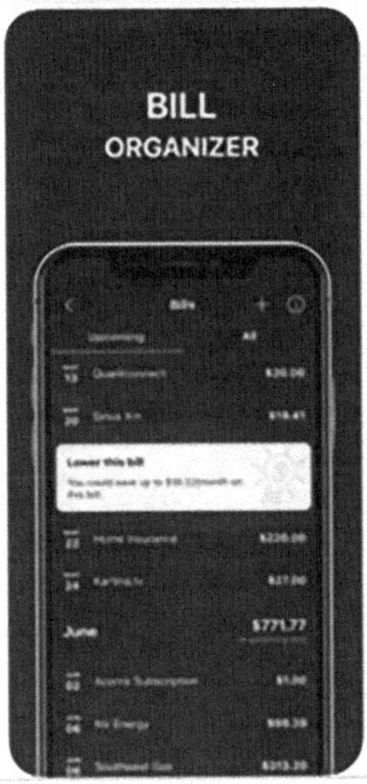

3. Greenlight

This is an app for the whole family with special features for kids and teens like children's debit cards, financial games that make learning money concepts easy, and so on. It helps you save, invest, and track expenses and helps build healthy financial habits with parental supervision.

You can start investing with as little as a dollar. It also allows parents to set chores for you around the house and to transfer payments for completed tasks to you automatically. It's a simple, fun app, and I would recommend you start with it.

Here are some screenshots for you to understand the app better:

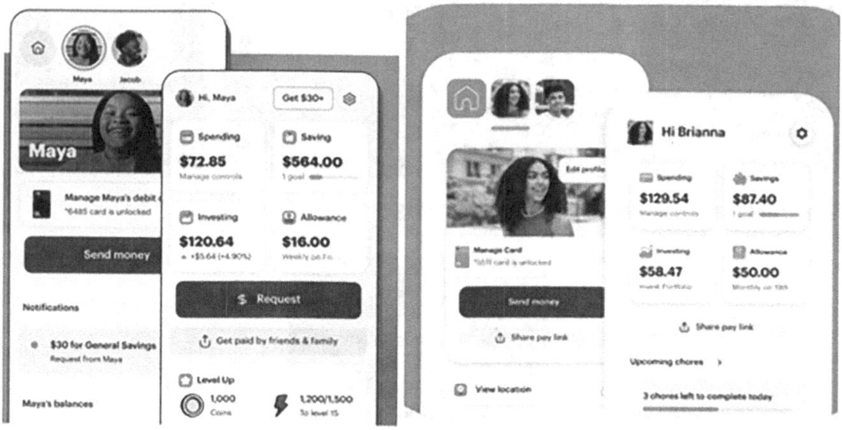

There are a few other apps too, like:

- Quicken
- You Need a Budget
- Monarch
- Nerd wallet
- Rocket money
- Every dollar

Most mobile apps are very user-friendly and self-explanatory, and you will be guided on account creation and features.

Alrighty, then! Let's put what we have learned into action. It's time for some activity.

Activity #1: Match the following financial terms to their correct definitions

Term	Definition
Overdrawing	An account where you deposit money to withdraw for daily expenses
Checking Account	A card that allows you to withdraw cash from ATMs and make purchases by swiping
Savings Account	Withdrawing more money than you have in your account
Debit Card	A spending plan for a month or year based on your income and expenses
Budget	An account that pays slightly higher interest rates, and is used to accumulate money

Activity #2: Download any money management app of your choice and track your expenses for one week.

Activity #3: Open a Mock Bank Account and Make a few Transactions for practice

This is one of the sites that lets you do this: https://message.bankofamerica.com/onlinebanking_demo/mobileApp_Simulator/

However, you can also look for sites on your own and practice.

Now, write about your experience here:

____

____

____

____

____

____

Now that you've got the basics of banking, you're well on your way to financial success. Up next, we'll explore advanced strategies to maximize your financial potential.

★★★

Part 2

Quest for Cash: Earning and Saving

So, we have discussed a lot of stuff about budgeting, bank accounts, and whatnot. But we've merely scratched the surface so far. It's time that we dive into the whole money-making shebang and see in detail the many different ways that you can not only earn your money, but also save it, and make it grow. We will take a look at simple investments that you can make as a teenager, and become a responsible and productive member of society.

Did you know that your country's defense programs, welfare programs, sports programs, and more, are all funded by the tax dollars citizens pay? Don't you think it's exciting to be able to contribute to your country, while also making money and building a nest egg for later in life?

Well, that's exactly what you're going to explore in the next two chapters. So put on your seatbelts, it's going to be a zippy ride!

Chapter 4

From Chores to Cha-Ching: Earning Strategies

Introduction to Earning Money

We took a sneak peek at the different ways that you can earn money as a teen, manage it, and even make it grow so that you can start planning for your adult and even retired life. Now we're going to take a closer look at those paths.

Why It's Important to Earn Money Yourself

Earning your own money is incredibly satisfying and fulfilling. I guarantee, that it'll make you feel so good about yourself inside that it'll be worth the hard work you put in to earn it.

Earning your own money also means learning about taxes. When you earn above a certain amount, you'll need to file taxes with the government. This might seem complicated, but it's a crucial part of being a responsible citizen. Don't worry, there are resources and tools to help you understand and file your taxes correctly.

You will realize the value of money when you have to work for it – unlike when you just get it from your parents. The sense of freedom that comes with earning your own money is something else altogether. It also teaches you to be a lot more responsible as an individual.

It's human nature, not to value things we get for free. But something we work hard for, something earned with our sweat—that, we truly understand the value of. I bet that you will feel a sense of pride when you buy things with money you earned, unlike your friends who've got it on a platter. You will earn their respect, along with your family's.

Well, I think that it's time to dive deeper and check out those methods in a little more detail. Shall we?

There are Many Creative Ways to Earn Money

a. Restaurants

Whether you're flipping burgers at McDonald's, making foamy hearts at a café, waiting tables in a diner, or scooping ice creams at a stand, being in the food industry is a great option for part-time work. Many restaurants also let you have a meal, so you can save on food.

b. Chores

Start at home and work your way around the neighborhood – mow lawns, take the trash out, shovel snow out of driveways, walk dogs, babysit kids, babysit pets, and basically help people with jobs they are unable to do themselves. It may not pay as well as the former, but it's still money.

c. College Jobs

If you're at Uni there's a wide choice when it comes to part-time jobs, like in the library, bookstore, gift store, and so on. Some standalone colleges also have these jobs on offer. The best part about these jobs is that you don't have to leave your campus for that. If you can find work in an eatery or café on campus, that's a double bonanza!

d. Gigs

Do you have any special talents? Singing, acting, crafts, drawing, painting, photography, modeling, sculpting, sewing, playing a musical instrument, dubbing or doing voice-over, or so on? Get on Craigslist or similar sites and advertise your availability for projects or gigs. You can sing in nightclubs or restaurants on the weekends or late evenings; this won't interfere with your classes.

e. Freelancing

If you are a wordsmith and can captivate readers with your writing, look for freelance writing jobs that you can do at your own pace. You can also start your own blog; choose a specific niche, and write regularly; a little savvy marketing, and you can get some loyal followers. You could try sites like Fiverr or Upwork to offer services like writing, graphic design, or social media management. It could be travel, the environment, food, animals – whatever interests you.

f. Car Care

Love 'em wheels? Then you'll enjoy this! Offer car wash services – at the customer's doorstep. All you've got to invest in is some gloves, car cleaning solutions, maybe some wax (charge extra for that), sponges, microfiber cloth, and a car vacuum. If your business takes off, invest in a power washer for quicker cleaning.

g. Home Baker

Everyone loves a good muffin, cookie, or brownie! If you have your own apartment which comes with its own oven, just invest in a few baking pans, and basic equipment. Make digital flyers that don't cost you anything, and share them on your socials. Bake according to orders and have them delivered – now that's a smart cookie!

h. Social Influencer

Are you good at making reels? Dancing, acting, singing? If you have a talent for the latter but not the former, you can always learn. Just go to YouTube and check out tutorials. You are likely to find plenty. This is just one resource. There are many more. Download apps like Canva, Photoshop, and InShot, and you will soon be making reels like a pro and posting them on Instagram.

You can also be a vlogger or video blogger; make videos on the topic that you're passionate about, and upload them on YouTube. Once your followers cross a certain level, you'll be able to monetize them. Now this might take a little more time than doing the other jobs we've discussed, but the earning potential is a lot higher here.

i. Interning

Depending on your major, you could try to get a paid internship in certain offices. If you're attending law school, you could try a law firm; if you're in business school, a bank, a retail giant, or any business you fancy. This may take some time, so if you're interested in interning, I suggest you start sending feelers or checking the 'Wanted interns' ads a little early on. Interning will also be invaluable for you academically, as you will get to see the practical side of all the theories you learn in class.

j. Online Jobs

There's a lot of different ways you can earn legit money online. If you didn't know it before, well, you do so now. You can sell stuff; be a reseller or sell your own handmade products. You can participate in surveys – there are many genuine ones.

Now these guys often hand out vouchers instead of actual cash, but it's usually for useful stuff, like groceries or appliances, so it's all good. You can also get data entry jobs – these are no-brainers, but you can make some decent money.

If you're mad about gaming, hey, why not participate in tournaments and make a quick buck?

Mist play is a totally awesome app for this same thing; it's a loyalty program for Android mobile game players. You earn rewards and can exchange them for gift cards from Amazon, Starbucks, PayPal, Visa, Xbox, and Google Play.

There are even sites where you can make game skins and sell them. Not bad, huh? Here are some other online jobs that can make you money:

- Affiliate marketing, which is basically promoting products through your blogs, videos, and reels
- Managing social media handles for celebrities or organizations
- Building your own app – if you've got the tech chops
- Working as a virtual assistant.
- Be a beta tester or user tester for new apps being developed by big companies

You can also become an entrepreneur!

An Amazing Teen Entrepreneurial Success Story

Now I don't want to sound preachy and stuff, or someone who wants to stop you from having fun; no, not at all. This is the age that should be enjoyed. But you can also be responsible while having fun! And to drive home my point, let me tell you about a smart little girl named Maddie Bradshaw.

Maddie, aged 10, went shopping with her mom to find stuff to decorate her school locker, but she wasn't happy with the stores options. So then, a weirdo uncle of hers gave her 50 bottle caps from his old Coke machine and asked her to transform them into art. Soon, her imagination took wings. She not only decorated them but also attached magnets to them and put them on her locker. Soon, her classmates, then other school students wanted them too.

Two years later, she started making fun jewelry out of these bottle caps called 'Snap Caps', and made unique pendants to represent each girl's individual personality. Did you know that in just one year, that is, when she was 13, she made her first million? She went on to participate in the reality show Shark Tank, got three 'sharks' to invest in her business, and expanded her business further.

What a simple idea it was, and what a success she made out of it! If she could do it, so can you. Of course, not every idea may turn out to be successful, but you can definitely give it a shot. And let's not forget that she started out with just a few hundred dollars – money that was given during festivals from relatives, or earned doing simple chores around the house.

The lesson to learn here is that even with a small initial capital, you can set start your entrepreneurial journey if you have an innovative idea, and if you can manage your money smartly. Maddie was smart; instead of spending her allowance on unnecessary stuff, she saved it to buy things she could make more money out of. Now she can afford to comfortably spend on her wants too.

Do you know of other ways to earn money? I would love to hear them. Drop me an email at dom_1984dec@hotmail.com.

Negotiate An Allowance and Become A Responsible Employee

You have to be smart about your allowance. Your parents are pretty likely to give you some handouts regardless of whether you do anything or not – after all, you will need money for your lunch and stuff. That's the bare minimum you are going to get if you're not enterprising.

The Fine Art of Negotiation

Now, you may think negotiations are only for business people, politicians, or well, hostage situations. But I kid you not if you know how to negotiate, you can make your life so much better. Think of it as a game! Here are some tips to negotiate well:

- Always check with your parents if it's a good time to talk, as you have something important to discuss; if they say no, ask them when it would be convenient for them.
- Make sure you're calm and have all your facts ready
- Make your request – first talk about why you need a higher allowance, and then your offer to do more chores
- You can even ask them for help with your schedule – for example, the day you planned to do the laundry may not be good for them; reschedule by agreeing on a day that's good for both of you.

Offer to do more chores around the house, and ask for a higher allowance. You can actually make a presentation using PowerPoint or Canva, and tell them what you are willing to do. It could include:

- Taking out the trash
- Doing the dishes
- Vacuuming
- Washing the car
- Doing laundry

- Mowing the lawn (if applicable)
- Babysitting your younger siblings when parents go out
- Organizing the closets
- Cleaning the bathroom
- Caring for your pets – including feeding, grooming, and walking them

You can create a schedule so that it's easy for you and your parents to keep track of what's being done. A spreadsheet is a great idea. Set reminders on your phone so that you don't miss a task.

You can set a specific price for each chore that you're willing to do. Now it's quite likely that your parents won't agree to everything you say – especially about the money they have to pay you. So, there are some things you have to promise and take care of at your end. For example:

- Set a timeline – say you will take out the trash between 5 to 6 pm on trash collection days; you will do the laundry on Saturdays, from 10 to 11.30 am, and so on
- Promise that you will do a thorough job, and KEEP that promise.
- In case you're pressed for time, say because you've got a test or an important basketball game coming up, tell the family in advance, and say you will make up for it later.
- If your parents think you're asking for too much, tell them that they can pay you a lower allowance in the beginning. Let them observe how well you're doing the chores for two weeks, and then pay you what you asked for.

Most of whatever you promise your parents is what you have to do if you get a part-time job outside, say at a restaurant, or convenience store. You have to be punctual; make sure you reach your work on time, and do your work honestly and sincerely.

Your employer must be able to rely on you, not keep worrying about why you haven't reached, or whether you're doing your job properly when they are not there. This is in a sense, preparing for the real world when you have to work full-time. The sooner you develop great habits at work, the better and more valued an employee you will become.

As we saw earlier, your work should not come at the cost of your studies. Don't take on too much work so that you're unable to handle your academics or other school activities. Your primary focus must be school/college, and this has to be secondary.

The trick is to use your free time productively – rather than wasting it just browsing Instagram, or TikTok videos, use that time to do something that will earn you something. You can do this when you're commuting, so you don't have to miss out on doing stuff you enjoy!

Resume Writing Tips

Well, you definitely don't need this at home, but when you apply for jobs outside – even if it is at a fast-food joint, you will need to submit a resume. There are a lot of templates available online. And people have different opinions about what makes a resume great. But here are some common details you need:

- Begin with your career objective
- Mention any previous job experience, starting from the most recent
- Mention any volunteer activities
- Write about your education, starting from the highest qualification
- Talk about extra-curricular activities
- Soft skills (public speaking, teamwork, etc.)
- IT skills

- Awards and prizes won
- Languages spoken

Acing Interviews

You will have to face an interview at almost any job you apply to. There's nothing to be nervous about. Find out what you can about your employer, and get a basic idea about their business model and values.

Most likely they will ask you a few standard questions like why you want the job, what you're good at, what you're not so great at, why they should hire you, whether are you a team player, and so on. Most employers start by asking you about yourself. They may be interested in knowing your goals in life, and what you have achieved in life so far.

The best thing to do is to be honest in your responses. Don't copy-paste your answers from some random website. There are no correct answers, just genuine ones!

It's activity time!

1. **In this worksheet, jot down your earning strategy, including part-time work, side hustles, and home chores.**

Job/Hustle	No. of hours per week	Wages

2. Do a SWOT analysis of yourself:

My Strengths	My Weaknesses
Opportunities I have	Threats to my Job (e.g – other teens)

Great, you're all set! You are empowered with the knowledge of how to make money, now it's time to get the low-down on how you cannot just save it, but watch it grow.

☆☆☆

Chapter 5

Saving Secrets of the Super Teen

So, you couldn't resist those cool shoes because they were on sale, huh? But they were still too steep for you, weren't they? And now, you don't have enough dough to go on the school trip? I get it, the offer was too good to pass up. But the thing you need to ask yourself is: were they really necessary at this time? What was more important - the trip or the shoes?

Your answer should be the trip; because travel, whether abroad or within your own state, creates amazing memories that will last you a lifetime, and teach you a great deal about life. Shoes, well, you can always get them the next time they go on sale, can't you?

a. Savings

As a very young kid, you were probably given a piggy bank, in which you could put coins that your parents or aunts and uncles gave you on festivals and birthdays. Well, you've surely outgrown those now. It's time for you to employ more grown-up methods to save!

We've already talked about bank accounts and why they are important in your savings journey, so we won't go over that again. Just a quick recap. A checking account is for your daily expenses, and a savings account helps you build your cash reserves so that you can have a substantial amount when you need it at a later stage.

b. Investment Options

There are a number of places you can invest money as a teenager. But before you actually get into the investment game, it's essential you know your risk appetite. That is, how okay you are with losing money, and how much money are you willing to gamble? Though not akin to gambling in a casino, investing in the stock market is a bit of a gamble! The higher the risk, the higher the reward. There are many 'safe' investments, but they will get you lower returns.

- *Your Own Business*

Do you have a solid idea for a business? Do you think it will work? If you're pretty sure you can make a success out of it – and this has to be after making a careful study and not just a hunch – launch your own business and become an entrepreneur! It doesn't have to be anything huge. But if you have an innovative idea and a well-crafted plan, you may just score big time.

Let's look at this example:

Rachel Zeits was playing lacrosse as a 13-year-old when her lacrosse rebounder got damaged badly. Looking at the gaping hole, she came up with an idea. She increased the thickness of the net and the steel bars, creating a super-durable lacrosse rebounder. Thanks to her smart idea, she made a cool million bucks just two years later, when she was just 15!

- *Custodial Accounts*

This is a type of account where an adult, usually the parent or guardian of a minor, makes the investments for the minor – in this case, you. This is until you turn 18, or in some states, 21.

These accounts are an amazing way of transferring assets to teens, while the custodian adult has legal responsibility, and the final decision is, of course, theirs. Custodial accounts are opened under the UGMA (Uniform Gifts to Minors Act) and the UTMA (Uniform Transfers to Minors Act).

If you're serious about starting to plan your retirement life right away, you can have a custodial Roth IRA or Roth individual retirement account. But – there's a teeny requirement – you need to have your own income to be able to have this account.

That means if you have any job, gig, hustle, or freelance work for which you get paid, only then can you participate in this. Teens can also have legal ownership along with an adult with specific joint brokerage accounts, and you can play a more active role here, though the final decision has to be approved by the adult who is the co-owner of the account.

- *Certificates of Deposit*

CDs are similar to savings accounts but there is a lock-in period, for which time you cannot touch the money in that account. It's the safest investment option for teens; while it doesn't get you exciting returns like the ones below, it will pay you more interest than your normal savings account. This is considered a conservative investment instrument with a low-risk profile. I would call it no-risk!

- *US Savings Bonds*

By far, the SAFEST investment you can make as a teenager. When you invest in a US Savings Bond, you're basically lending money to the US Government. Isn't that something? They are not as lucrative as stocks, but uber-safe. You don't have to worry about the market crashing and losing your money. The Series EE Bonds and Series I Savings Bonds pay interest for up to 30 years, and it's a sure thing. The interest rate on the series I bond is adjusted from time to time, allowing for inflation.

- *Mutual Funds*

Unlike stocks that are of a single company, funds are invested in multiple stocks and various other assets, depending on goals that are defined in the fund's prospectus. A mutual fund is managed by a professional money manager and does carry some risk, but here, thanks to diversification, the risk is spread, unlike in stocks of single companies.

- *Exchange-Traded Funds*

ETFs are another safe option for you to put your money in. They represent a diverse group of companies and are traded like stocks – quite like mutual funds – and can be bought through your broker. Look at the NASDAQ, Dow Jones, and such broad market indices to know which specific ETFs you should invest in. ETFs are designed to track specific sectors, market indexes, or other assets.

- *Stocks*

Make a list of companies you're interested in. Maybe Nike because you're into sports; Netflix because you stream content; Apple because, well, you're a fan of their devices. Read their annual reports or 10 Ks, and get an idea of how well your favorite companies are doing, what they're doing, and so on.

Check out Yahoo! Finance, Stockanalysis.com, and Market Watch to get an unbiased view of how well these companies are doing. You can then shortlist one or two companies and invest in their stocks – become a shareholder. Shareowners get dividends as announced by the company each year; the dividend depends on how well the business is going. A shareholder is a part owner of the company, so you are entitled to get a part of the profits – how cool is that?

- *Cryptocurrency*

Ah, the mysterious instrument of investment! Let's take a moment to understand cryptocurrency. Think of it as virtual money that you can buy and sell on an encrypted network. This network is called the block chain. Now, cryptocurrency can also be used to purchase many goods and services.

Keep in mind that this is completely virtual and has no physical existence whatsoever. No government in the world issues it either. There are different types of cryptocurrency, like Bit coin, Ethereum, Doge, Solana, Ripple, and AVAX. In fact, there are thousands of cryptocurrencies, but not all have good market value.

Many financial experts consider cryptocurrency to be the future of finance, which means, you must know about it.

Legally, anyone can invest in cryptocurrency, but most crypto exchanges in the US mandate that users must be a minimum of 18 years old. Cryptocurrency is unregulated and is a high-risk, high-reward investment, and anyone who wants to invest in it must exercise due diligence and caution, as with any high-risk investment option.

Cryptocurrencies are traded on centralized exchanges like Binance. US, Coin base, and so on. You deposit dollars and buy crypto. It's a very volatile investment, and the value tends to swing to either extreme.

Some Things to Remember About Investment:

- Don't be in a rush to multiply money. Slow and steady wins the race. Start small and let it grow slowly.
- Diversify your investments; don't put all your money in one type of investment. Spread your investment across stocks, funds, bonds, and other instruments. When you invest in stocks, be sure to buy stocks of different companies.
- Get basic knowledge about stocks, how the markets work, inflation, interest rates, and more.
- Learn what companies do, how they do it, how much money they make, how much dividend and interest they pay out, and how popular their stocks are.
- Play around with dummy portfolios to familiarize yourself with stocks and investing.
- Don't fall for get-rich-quick schemes. If something sounds too good to be true, it probably is!
- Select the ideal custodial brokerage account; depending on your state, you may need to be 18 or 21 to invest in financial instruments. Check out online brokers like

Fidelity, E-Trade, Ally Invest, Stash, Stockpile, and Charles Schwab.

- Higher returns always mean higher risks.
- The stock market is volatile – just like a bubbling pot, and you never know when it may crash or spike; you should invest in stocks after careful consideration, and don't invest too much anyway.
- Avoid penny stocks – companies whose stocks trade for under $5.
- Don't invest in companies that are unknown, or deal with brokers you've never heard of before.
- For more investing tips, you can follow TeenVestor.com, Teen Business (a YouTube channel), and Investor.gov, run by the SEC.

Leverage The Power of Compound Interest

You may have been wondering how this works! You've already seen how your bank pays you interest when you put money in a savings account, right? Now this interest can be put back into the savings account, along with the original deposit, and you can earn interest on that. In this way, you will see that if you leave your money in a savings bank account untouched for a while, you can make your money grow in a huge way.

Say you've put $500 in a savings account, and at the end of the first year, you get $20 as interest. This is also put into the savings account, so your deposit amount for the second year is $520, and you will earn interest on this amount at the end of the second year. *(This is not an actual calculation, but just an illustration to help you understand)*

Take help from family, and find out how long it will take for your money to double in various investments. There is something called the Rule of 72; let's say that the return on an investment is 9%. Divide 72 by 9, and you get 8. That's the number of years in which the money you have invested in that instrument, will double. So, if you have invested $2,500 in that particular source, in 8 years, you will get $5000. If you continue to put the interest earned back into that instrument, you will earn interest on that as well, and your eventual returns will be pretty high. Look for investment options that yield higher returns, but remember that these will also be riskier.

Here's an illustration that makes it easier to understand at a glance:

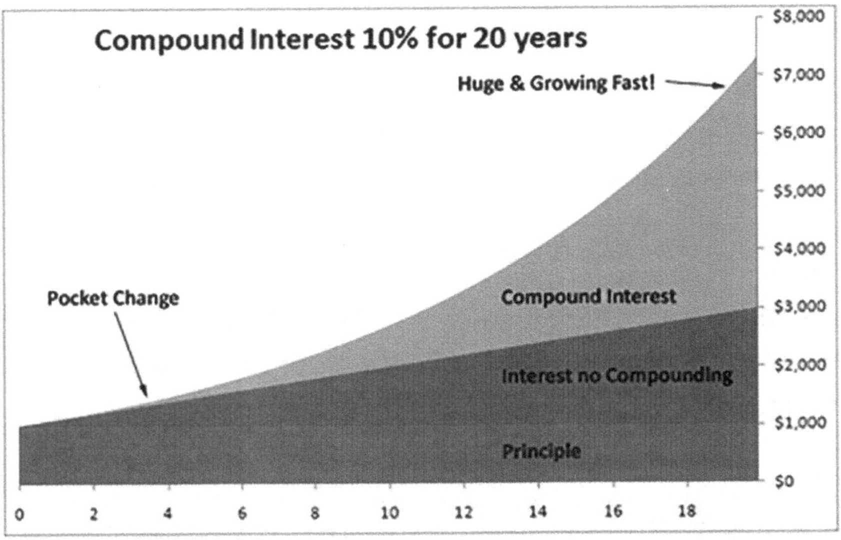

If you want to check out for yourself how much your money will grow with compound interest, here is a site that you can try: The Calculator Site. Enter the currency, amount, interest rate, and the period of your choice, and see how much money you will have at the end. You can play around with different combinations that will help you see how your money choices impact your savings.

For example, you can even input stuff like additional deposits to add to your principal amount, withdrawals for certain needs, and so on.

You can also check out the official US government site Investor.gov. It's not as much fun as the previous one, since it's an official site, but you can be assured of accurate results. It also has a lot of information about savings and investments, and a savings goal calculator and other tools, but some of it could be a bit heavy for you.

#1. Make a portfolio where you want to invest

Type of Investment	Rate of Return	Amount to Invest

 # 2. Make a list of companies you like, and find out online the dividend they have paid on their shares in the last financial year:

Company Name	Rate of Dividend

Filling this table will give you a clearer picture of which company's stocks to invest in.

3. Track the progress of your savings or investment goals:

Goal #	Progress at 3 months	Progress at 6 months	Progress at 9 months	Progress at 12 months
Save $800 for a Macbook	Saved $ 120	Saved $300	Savings $ 430	Saved $ 675

This will help you keep track of how well you are working towards that goal. I have filled in the first one to make it simpler for you. (It's not based on a real calculation). Of course, you may have short-term goals too, which you may reach by the time you complete 3 to 6 months. If you're really determined and work hard, hey, you may very well be able to buy that MacBook within 9 months!

Okay then! You've got your plan to make money and save it, and you've taken the first few steps towards financial success. It's time now for us to look at ways to manage your money smartly so that you make the right choices and achieve your goals.

☆☆☆

Part 3

Financial Fitness: Making Smart Choices

Now that we have spoken about how to make money, manage it, make it grow, make a budget, use the right tools to invest it wisely, and more, it's time to move on to stuff like debt; how you can manage it, avoid it, pay it off, and more. Are you ready? Let's get started.

Chapter 6

Debt Decoder: Friend or Foe?

Drake Bell, once one of the biggest child stars on Nickelodeon channel, filed for bankruptcy in 2014 – he said he owed $581,000. Bell was earning $2,820 per month but was spending over $18,000 – can you imagine? His home in LA went into foreclosure, and he lost it. His house was worth 2 million US dollars, and he had to sell it off for much less.

What a sorry state of affairs for someone who was at one time, rich and famous! So, how did this come about? The only way anyone can rack up so much debt is because of reckless spending. No budgeting, no tracking, and impulse purchases – the (un)holy trifecta!

Granted, everyone, or almost everyone, has some debt. Do you think any debt at all is bad? Some people think so. I don't; I prefer to categorize debt as good or bad. It all depends on the way you use the money you borrow, the repayment terms, and whether the debt has any benefits for you or not.

I. What Is Good Debt?

Good debt helps you achieve important goals, or give you long-term financial gain.

Examples:

1. Student Loans

Taking a loan for a degree or vocational course sets you on course for a profession. You may have to borrow higher amounts for, say, med school or law school, but you're charting your course to a lucrative career.

2. Mortgages

Homeownership offers satisfaction, security, and stability, and is a means of building wealth. As you pay off the loan, you build equity, or ownership in that property.

3. Business Loans

You may have a great business idea but no cash to invest – you may need to rent space, buy equipment, or hire staff. Business loans are available for this purpose; as they are used to start or grow a business, which can bring in more money, it can be seen as a good loan.

4. Interest-free Loans

These are available to students, small business owners, and homeowners, say to make sustainable home improvements.

5. Refinanced debt

You can refinance your existing loan with a lender who is willing to offer you more favorable terms of payment.

II. What Is Bad Debt?

You could say that a loan taken for unproductive uses – one that will not yield any money to the borrower in the future, is a bad debt. Let's look at a few examples:

Credit card debt

These usually have very high interest rates, so if you don't pay your outstanding amount each month, that can be a bad debt.

High-interest loans

Loans that carry high interest rates are to be avoided at all costs.

Personal Loan/Discretionary Spending Loan

Loans that are taken for vacations, branded clothes, accessories, cosmetics, or hobbies.

It's best to avoid these types of loans; avoid borrowing when it's not really necessary. This can lead you into a debt trap, where you keep taking new loans to pay your previous ones.

III. Loan Terms and Interest Rates

Here are some words you should be familiar with:

- **Down Payment** – An initial payment you need to make when you're buying something substantial, like a car, on loan
- **Tenure** – The period you have availed the loan for – 12 months, 6 months, 24 months, etc.
- **EMI** – The equated monthly installments are the payments you need towards the loan every month. This amount includes a principal component and an interest component.
- **Interest Rate** – This is the cost you have to bear to borrow money. It is usually shown as a percentage – 7% interest on a student loan, for example.
- **Pre-Closure** – If you have the funds and want to pay off the loan before its closure date, you can.
- **Processing Fee** – The fee charged by the lender to process your loan; it could be around 1-2% of the loan amount
- **Non-payment or Default or Delinquency** – I think it's pretty self-explanatory! The lender will charge a fine if you default on your payment.

Loan terms refer to the conditions on which the bank gives you loans; it is usually included in a document. The bank will mention everything, including the amount, tenure, interest rate, your EMI, and all the conditions, fees, and charges we discussed above.

Here are a few things you need to keep in mind where loans are concerned:

- The higher the loan amount, the higher your monthly payments
- The longer the duration, the more interest you end up paying; that is, the cost of borrowing money is high, even though your monthly payments may be less
- The higher your initial payment, the lower your monthly payments and total interest burden.

Understanding Credit Scores

What is a credit score? Think of it like your report card where your financial health is concerned! Your credit score is expressed as a three-digit number, and it tells the lenders how savvy and responsible you are with money. This score is granted by independent credit rating agencies.

The higher your score, the better; a high score tells a prospective lender that you're highly likely to repay a loan in time, not default on your monthly payments, and so on. They will be more inclined to offer you a loan or credit card.

Now how is this score calculated? The credit rating agency will review your credit history, loan repayment history, credit card usage, how much you currently owe, the length of your history, types of credit used, and new credit.

If you have a high credit score, you may also be offered lower interest rates, credit cards with attractive offers, and even certain jobs. Building a positive credit history from an early age is a smart idea.

IV. Not Sure if it's Good or Bad Debt

Well, sometimes, it may be tough to decide if a debt is good or bad.

Take credit card debt, for instance. Usually seen as a bad debt, it's not really bad if you pay the full outstanding amount every month. If you have a card with a 0% introductory APR offer, you can pay off your outstanding bills over a period of time without paying interest.

Moreover, if you use a credit card and pay your bills on time, you can start building an impressive credit history – as we saw earlier, a high credit score can get you loans on favorable terms, jobs, and even help you rent an apartment.

Buy Now Pay Later or BNPL schemes allow you to buy stuff and pay your bill over a specific time without interest. However, be careful not to go haywire and buy too many things through BNPL – you're sure to land in hot water!

So, you see, it all depends on how you're going to use the money, whether the debt is good or bad.

How to Avoid Bad Debt

Ah, now we come to the most important part. Look at our child star, Drake; should he have bought a home in LA for two million dollars? Probably not! He could have bought a smaller one, invested the rest in mutual funds or bonds, and multiplied his money instead.

Often, bad debts are a choice and can be easily avoided. For example, an expensive car, the latest phone, or big-label clothes; you can always wait till you have saved up enough. On the other hand, you may have been forced to take a high-interest loan for your education or an unforeseen medical emergency.

However, it could be possible to avoid this bad debt in both types of situations if you create a budget. This will let you see where you're spending more than necessary, and come up with ways to save money. (As discussed earlier.)

We also briefly touched upon putting money in a savings account, so that you can have a substantial stash when you need it for say, buying a car, or some kind of emergency. Ideally, your emergency fund should be about 3-6 months' worth of your living expenses.

So, if you spend $1,000 every month, you should have $6,000 saved up and kept for emergency use. This can help you avoid taking on bad credit.

You can qualify for lower-interest loans and credit cards with amazing benefits if you build a good credit score. You can build your credit score by paying off your outstanding card balances and other monthly payments in time.

How to Get Out of Debt

Have you made a few bad decisions and are now feeling overwhelmed with debt? Don't worry. There's always a way out. Here are some steps to take immediately.

1. Organize Your Debts

Make a list of all your loans and credit card debts, along with the amounts.

2. Compare Strategies

Look at different tactics and compare them to see which one you find the most doable. Do you want to pay off the loan with the highest rate of interest (debt avalanche strategy), or do you want to focus on the account with the lowest balance (debt snowball strategy)?

Maybe you want to combine all your debts into a single new loan that has a lower interest rate or EMI than what you have now. This is called debt consolidation. It can make your payments a lot simpler, and you can also save money on the interest you have to pay.

Your choice will depend on how much cash you have left in your budget at the end of the month, and your credit.

3. Prioritize

To get out of debt, you need to make some hard decisions. You may need to tighten your belt, cut luxuries - and even few necessities, or find new ways to make money so that you have enough to pay off the outstanding amounts.

I agree, it's challenging, but hey, you will be much better off in the near future, if you do this, trust me.

4. Get Support

If you feel too overwhelmed or are unable to make your budget work, you can get professional help. A financial counselor can help you to understand your financial habits and control your spending.

Nonprofit credit counselors can help with budget creation and optimization. They can help you set up a debt management plan, whereby the counselor helps you negotiate and save money. You can get your monthly payments reduced as well.

Financial assistance programs can help pay for necessities so that you can use the money saved to pay off debts.

5. A Few Hard Decisions

If it's near impossible to pay off debts, consider this:

Settling your debts: By negotiating with the credit card company, you may be able to pay less than the outstanding and settle the balance. While this can impact your credit score, it is better than leaving debts unpaid.

A word of caution, though: This should not be your go-to plan; it should be the last resort, only if you are completely overwhelmed by debt.

How Do Students Accumulate Debt?

Ever wondered why students rack up unpaid bills? Let's take a look.

According to Pew Research, students from college-educated families, usually have automobile loans – around 43%, and credit card debt – 60%. The pattern is similar among students from less educated homes.

The study also says that the average college student has a total debt that equals two years of the family income, at 205%! Less educated families with student debt have total debts that equal a year's total family income.

One in six teenagers and young adults is finding it difficult to repay their debt burden; since 2009-2010 student debt has overtaken credit card debt in the US. Many students are more than six months late on their payments, and this could badly impact their credit scores, making it difficult to apply for a loan in the future.

Now here's the thing: we all know, that in a country like the US, it can be difficult to get to your classes or work without a car. A car is a necessity, I'll grant you that. What you need to be careful about is which car to buy.

You can buy a car for just a couple of thousand dollars – which means you may need a very small loan – or for tens of thousands of dollars. Buying a used car, small and functional, will do the job just as well as a brand-new, expensive one, for which you will need to take out a huge loan.

Loan delinquencies can smear your credit scores badly, as can being behind on your credit card payments for over 30 days. Avoid both!

Responsible Borrowing

Now don't get me wrong, I'm not saying that you can live your whole life without ever borrowing money for anything. I would be kidding if I said that! I have borrowed money, too.

The trick is to be a **responsible and smart** borrower. The golden rule is to avoid borrowing money to fund unnecessary expenses. That should be your mantra.

The second thing to remember is to only borrow what you actually need, and what you can pay back comfortably. Never borrow simply to have a good time. Trust me, it's not worth it in the end.

And third, always be responsible and pay your debts off on time. Set up automated payments from your checking account so that you don't have to physically go and do it. Just make sure you have enough cash in your account.

Fixed Vs. Variable Interest Rates.

If your bank charges a fixed interest rate, it means that the interest rate remains unchanged for the entire duration of the loan. Most car loans and student loans are given on a fixed interest rate basis.

Variable interest rate means that the interest charge can go up or down according to the prevailing Federal Funds Rate, market conditions, and more. This is a dicey thing, as you don't know when the interest rates may go up. Sure, it's great if they come down, but there's no guarantee of that happening.

When the Federal rate goes up, you can earn more on your investments, and pay more interest on your debt.

Simple Vs. Compound Interest

Simple interest is the interest paid on the principal amount you have borrowed; it is also paid on your deposits.

Compound interest is the interest paid or levied on the principal plus the interest. So, while compound interest is great for your deposits, it's not good news for loans.

Understanding APR

You can compare loans by working out the APR or Annual Percentage Rate of the different loans; this will tell you which one will cost more. The interest rate, fees charged by lenders, and the repayment term are taken into consideration to calculate the APR.

One way to compare loans is to calculate the annual percentage rate (APR) of the various options to see which one will cost more on an annualized basis. A loan's APR considers the interest rate, certain fees, and repayment terms.

Here's an online APR calculator for you: https://www.calculatorsoup.com/calculators/financial/apr-calculator.php. This is what it looks like:

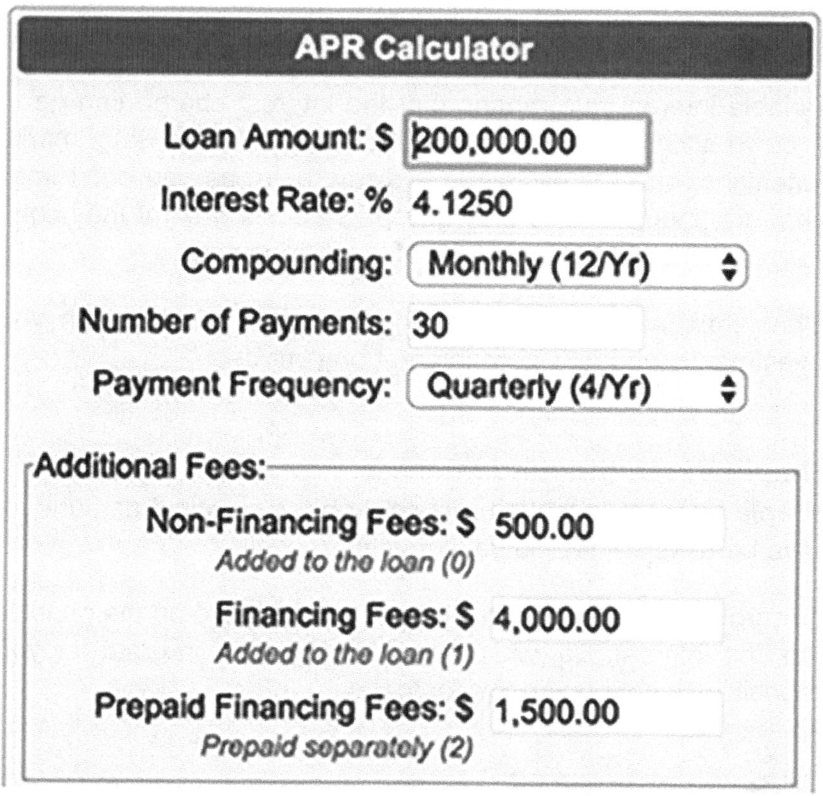

Ideally, a loan with an APR of over 10% should be avoided. Always look for loans with lower APRs; there are many banks and credit card companies out there. Do your research and compare them before you choose.

Avoiding Credit Card Pitfalls

Credit cards incur one of the highest interest rates of all debt, and can become difficult to manage at times.

According to a National Debt Relief study, students use up nearly all their credit limits; the average limit is around $3,500, and the credit card debt is around $3,300.

We saw some really scary stats about student credit card debt above. Credit cards can be very useful – to rent apartments, buy cars, and groceries, book flight tickets home, and whatnot. But be very careful to only charge your cards up to a certain percentage of your total available limit, and remember to pay the full outstanding amount each month.

Don't apply for too many credit cards; every time you submit an application for a credit card, the card company runs a credit check – and when this happens once too often, uh-oh, red flag!

Never ignore the fine print: there is a lot of information the card company puts on their website or application form where all the charges are mentioned. These may not be very obvious, but they are there, so you should read it, and understand how much you will end up paying if you're not careful about timely payment.

It's super easy to get carried away, and over-spend when you have a credit card. Many young people end up with a whole lot of stuff that they don't need – they just bought it because it was on sale, or because they had a credit card handy, and so on.

We spoke earlier about knowing the difference between needs and wants. You need to apply the same thought process here too. Avoid spending on wants – or at least, limit them severely. Save it for special occasions like birthdays or other celebrations. That's fine; everyone needs to splurge occasionally.

Some wants may turn into necessities. For example, you WANT a new phone, but there's nothing really wrong with your current one; it's just old. But let's say your phone falls into the water or gets damaged in some other way. Now you actually need a new phone – but here too, you should ask yourself if you really need a very high-end phone.

The danger happens when the splurging becomes the new normal – so don't ever let that happen.

Maxing out your credit cards can also deliver a knockout punch to your credit score! Credit rating agencies don't like it when you do that. Even so, if you pay off the entire balance on the due date, you will be okay.

Activity #1

List all your debts with the following details:

Loan/ Debt	Total Amount	Remaining Amount	EMI	Duration/ Tenure	Remaining Tenure	Interest Rate

I have kept the box small in the hope that you don't have a lot of different loans or out standings.

Activity #2

Make a list of things you want to buy – and against each item, mark it with Want or Need. If something is a need, explain to yourself why.

★★★

Chapter 7

Protecting Your Future

Introduction to Insurance

All this while, we have been talking about how to develop healthy money habits, how to make money, manage money, track and control your expenses, and invest money to make it grow. But have you ever wondered how you can keep everything safe – your investments, your car, and even yourself?

What exactly is insurance?

Hmm, well, think of the seat belt you wear for safety when you ride in a car; insurance is like a safety belt for your investments. It is important to know the basics of insurance so that you can protect yourself and your assets from day one.

Insurance can help cover unexpected damage to your car, your health, the people around you, and even your home (even as a tenant). You are required to pay a small amount called a premium, every year, for this benefit.

You may have to pay the premium monthly, quarterly, half-yearly, or yearly. The premium amount is calculated by the insurance company after considering many risk factors like your age, location, the value of the asset being insured, and so on.

When you buy insurance, you are securing your assets as you won't need to pay out of your pocket for loss or damage caused to them. When you've insured your car, let's suppose the first year was uneventful.

You renew the insurance and have a mild collision, and your car gets dented and scratched. Now you can get the car repaired through insurance. You may still need to pay a small amount, but compared to the actual cost, it's going to be peanuts.

How Does Insurance Work?

Whatever money you pay as a premium is put in a common pool along with the insurance premiums paid by the other customers of the company. A part of this money is used to pay for the operational costs of the company, some of it is invested in low-risk investments, and some is used to pay customers who have submitted claims.

Just like your investments, the insurance company's investments earn returns, making this money pool even bigger. It is thanks to these profits that the insurer can charge you lower premiums to cover potentially huge expenses when there is an emergency or accident.

Life is unpredictable, but insurance provides a cushion. You can avoid a lot of tension and be at peace when you have insurance. Some insurance is mandatory – required by law – while others are completely optional.

Let's take a moment to pause here; when we spoke about budgeting, we had mentioned the heads of expense for which you need to set money aside. Now that you have learned about insurance, it's another expense head you need to provide for.

a. Medical Insurance

Every person in the US is now legally required to have medical or health insurance. If you don't have it, you may have to pay a fine or penalty – and it's getting steeper every year. While the Affordable Care Act introduced an individual mandate, it has been effectively repealed, and there is no longer a federal penalty for not having health insurance. However, some states have their separate mandates.

You may think that you are young, a total fitness freak, and healthy as a horse, and that you're never going to fall sick; well at least not for the foreseeable future. Oh, but what if you had a fall? Got involved in an accident? Contracted a contagious illness? The medical expenses can burn a hole in your pocket all the way to the north pole!

How to buy Health Insurance

There are a number of ways to do this, and the costs and advantages differ. Check out the available options based on your age, health status, etc.

- **Parents' Plan:** You can be on your parents' health insurance plans till you turn 26 – that's a pretty long time. And, you can be married, be financially independent, or even live elsewhere, but this is still available to you.
- **COBRA:** The Consolidated Omnibus Budget Reconciliation Act of 1985 allows people to continue their existing health plan for a limited time, preventing sudden loss of coverage.
- **Short-term policy:** Some insurers let you purchase student or short-term insurance policies so that you are covered even if you have a gap between finishing school and landing your first job. These are more affordable than COBRA.
- **Employer plans:** It is the most affordable option as your employer pays for part of the insurance. While some employers may offer to cover your health from day one, others may first require you to work for a period of 30, 60, or even 90 days before the insurance kicks in.
- **Individual policy:** The most expensive option for you, as it is personalized and not shared; if you smoke or have an existing health condition, your premium is likely to be higher.
- **Medicaid:** Also called medical assistance, it is another government-funded health insurance offered to people with disabilities, with low income, and so on. You can find out if you qualify for Medicaid by enquiring with the HHD (Department of Health and Human Development) program in your state.
- **Subsidized State Program:** Uninsured individuals under 19 can get state help thanks to the State Children's Health

Insurance Program; provided that your family income falls below a specific range.

- **The Health Insurance Marketplace:** Here, people can choose the insurance that fits their requirements, and is also called Health Insurance Exchange.

What If I Have a Health Problem?

If you have asthma, diabetes, congenital heart disease, or a disability, you have what insurance companies call a 'pre-existing condition'. Though insurance companies are not permitted to deny insurance to people with pre-existing conditions, they may charge higher premiums to cover you.

What Type of Insurance Do I Need?

Well, that depends! You need to check and compare different plans to see what they cover and what they don't, and of course, how much each one costs. You will have to strike a balance between paying the minimum while ensuring that you have covered all your bases.

It's a good idea to look at everything the plan has, and not ONLY the cost – in this case, the premium. Say, you find a plan with a very low monthly premium. But the co-pay component may be very high in such a plan, or you may need to pay more money for prescriptions; which means it's not really as cheap as you think.

Then again, if you are generally in excellent health, you can consider such a plan to begin with. But if you need to see a doctor frequently, or need prescription medicines regularly, a plan that has higher premiums but covers more of the cost of your visits and medicines is actually more affordable in the end.

Another thing you need to make sure of is that the plan you want to buy covers the services that are important to you. If you need therapy or believe in alternative medicine like acupuncture, require dental care, and so on, make sure that your insurance provider is willing to cover the costs of such medical care.

There are three main types of plans that you most likely have to choose from. Let's see what they are:

a. *Indemnity Plans*

Reimbursement or fee-for-service plans let you consult the doctor of your choice at any time. In these plans, you pay the doctor directly and then submit a claim to the insurance company. They will reimburse you for a portion of the amount you paid.

Annual physicals and other preventive care measures are usually not covered by indemnity plans. They also tend to have higher premiums than other plans, as you get the freedom to choose your doctors.

b. *Managed Care Plans*

This is the type of plan you usually get when your health insurance is through your employer. Here the health insurance provider enters into a contract with certain doctors, hospitals, and labs, and gets them to provide healthcare to the insured members at a lower price. There are four types of managed care plans:

- **HMO or Health Maintenance Organization,** where you choose your primary care doctor when you join. This doctor coordinates your entire medical care, from annual exams to emergency hospitalization. The co-pay for these services is usually very low, but you can only use those hospitals and doctors who are approved by the plan. You also need a written referral to consult a specialist.
- **PPO or Preferred Provider Organization,** where you have a little more flexibility, letting you consult any doctor of your choice; however, your co-pay will be higher here.
- **POS or Point of Service plan,** where you choose a network doctor mostly, but can go out of the network to consult a specialist. When you do so, your co-pay component is likely to be higher.
- **EPO or Exclusive Provider Organization** Similar to a PPO, but with a smaller network of participating doctors.

c. *Consumer-Driven Health Plan (CDHP)*

This is fairly recently introduced and allows you to set aside a specific sum of money in a special account for health insurance savings. You can decide how to use this money for your healthcare expenses. You will most likely have higher deductibles or co-pay components in this plan compared to others.

Don't stress about this thinking that you're never going to use it, so why buy it? Simply think about buying health insurance as an investment in your health!

b. Car Insurance

This is probably the second most important type of insurance as far as you are concerned. If you want to drive a car, the law says that you must have insurance. There are many different types of coverage available, and it's important that you know all about it. Keep in mind that even though these are not all compulsory; some are optional.

1. ***Auto liability coverage***

This is mandatory almost throughout the US, and drivers must purchase at least the minimum amount of liability coverage as set by their state. Liability coverage is made up of:

- Bodily injury liability which can help pay the medical bills of someone you injure
- Property damage liability can help pay for the damage you cause to someone's property while driving.

2. ***Uninsured and underinsured motorist coverage***

Let's say it was your tough luck that you got hit by a driver without insurance; in such a case, uninsured motorist coverage can help pay your hospital bills or vehicle repairs.

If the driver has insufficient insurance – meaning they have insurance but the liability limit is too low to pay your medical bills, this insurance could help. This is a requirement in some states, but optional in others.

3. *Comprehensive coverage*

This type of insurance is optional, but it is good to have, as it can help cover the expenses if your own car gets damaged, stolen, vandalized, catches fire, and so on. Repairs and replacements up to the actual value of the car will be paid for by the insurer after deducting a pre-decided amount. This deductible is what you have to pay yourself.

4. *Collision coverage*

Let's say you collide with another vehicle, or an object like a wall or fence; this type of insurance can help with repairs or replacements to your car up to its actual value, after deducting a specific amount. It is optional, though the car's lender or leaseholder may require you to have it.

5. *Medical payments coverage*

In case you or a family member driving the insured car gets injured in an accident, this type of coverage can help to pay the medical bills like hospital visits, X-rays, surgery, and more. In some states this is optional, but in others it is mandatory.

6. *Personal injury protection*

Personal injury protection is not available in all states. It is similar to medical payment coverage, and you may get reimbursed for your accident-related medical expenses. Additionally, PIP may help to pay for incidental expenses due to the accident like loss of income. This too is not required in all states.

On top of these main types of coverage, you can add several options to your policy, like the following:

- Rental reimbursement coverage/transportation expense coverage to get a rental vehicle while your own car is getting repaired

- Gap coverage covers the difference between the outstanding on your can loan and the actual value of your car, which your insurer will pay if it is stolen or totaled.
- New car replacement cover to replace your car with a new car of the same make and model in case it was stolen or totaled within a set time (usually, two years or less)
- Towing and labor cost coverage can get you towing, gas service, lookout service, a new battery, and so on if you get stranded on the road.

You should check with your car dealer, local DMV office, family, and friends to know what insurance is required in your state. Compare different insurance companies: the services they offer, the premiums they charge, reviews left by other customers, and so on, and then decide on an insurance company to insure your car.

The insurance company may have certain requirements from you, like proper parking, electronic lock, alarm system, and so on. You are expected to take all essential precautions to protect your car from theft and damage.

c. Renter's Insurance

This is not mandatory insurance, but it's good to have. Also, your landlord may insist that you have a renter's policy so that in case you get your stuff stolen or damaged while you're renting their place, they can avoid problems.

If your landlord asks you to buy tenants' insurance, it's your responsibility to look for and finalize your insurance provider and coverage.

What to Expect in a Tenant's Policy

- **Personal property coverage** – can help replace your stuff that was stolen or damaged, say by fire. This includes furniture, clothing, accessories, computers, TVs, or other devices.

- **Liability coverage –** If you are held legally responsible for the injuries of a visitor or for damage to another person's property, this coverage can help cover the expenses. Let's say you forgot to close the faucet in the bathtub and the water flows out and down into the apartment below. This coverage can help you pay to repair the damage caused.
- **Additional living expenses coverage –** In case you have to leave your apartment because the building is damaged by fire or some other accident, this cover can help you pay for expenses like motel or hotel bills, which are temporary in nature.

You need to remember that these covers are likely to have limits, that is, they will specify the maximum amount of money the insurer will pay for a covered loss as per your policy. You will need to shell out some money. This deductible is what you agree to pay, in order for your insurance cover to be activated.

How much renter's insurance do I need?
This depends on the value of your belongings. How much does it all cost – your clothes, accessories, electronics, and any other stuff you bought yourself? A smart thing to do would be to document all that you own and how much cash you would need to replace it all.

This method will help you choose the proper amount of tenant insurance coverage you need.

Insuring your Savings and Investments

Now you know how to protect your health and your car; but what about your money? Can you insure that? How do you provide safety for your hard-earned savings and investments? Let's find out!

The FDIC or Federal Deposit Insurance Corporation protects savings deposits up to a limit of $250,000. Your securities market investments had no protection at all till 1970 when Congress established the SIPC or Securities Investor Protection Corporation.

The SIPC protects investors like you against losses you may incur because of broker bankruptcies; however, you do NOT have insurance against losses due to regular market transactions or frauds. Investors are reimbursed up to $500,000, including $250,000 in cash in case a member firm becomes insolvent. You will also get back any securities that are currently registered in the certificate form in your name.

What this means is that if you've invested more than $30,000 in cash with a broker who then becomes insolvent, you will lose $50,000.

Therefore, you could say that the SIPC functions as a trustee and recovers assets if and when a dealer or broker becomes insolvent. It oversees the recovery process to ensure that customers' claims are paid without delay or fuss.

Here, the term 'member firms' is important; those broker firms that are members of the SIPC only are covered. So if your broker or dealer isn't an SIPC member and they become insolvent, then it's tough luck.

What About Investment Losses?

When you invest in stocks, mutual funds, bonds, and so on, there is always risk involved; a certain uncertainty. There is no protection or insurance that you can get for the loss you may incur in such investments. Some people invest in rare whiskies, art, and other collectibles, but the insurance only covers theft or damage from fire, etc., and not the value coming down (depreciation).

You see, the whole idea about investing is the risk involved; ergo, you cannot insure your investments. The riskier the investment, the higher you stand to gain – whether it's interest, dividends, capital gains, or anything else.

The lower the risk, the lower the returns you get; certain investments guarantee safety for your principal or initial investment, but they usually offer pretty low returns.

Currently, you can only minimize the risk of losses in the stock market by diversifying your investments – spreading them across a variety of assets, so that your losses in one investment can be offset by gains in another.

The Role of the SEC

The Securities and Exchange Commission deals with fraud and other losses, as does the FINRA or Financial Industry Regulatory Authority.

Regulatory agencies such as the Securities and Exchange Commission (SEC) and the Financial Industry Regulatory Authority (FINRA) deal with issues related to fraud and other losses.

That's about all that you need to know as far as insurance is concerned. As you grow older, you will need to purchase insurance for your home when you become an owner, and so on.

FUN FACT: By the way, did you know that athletes often insure their legs, singers their voices, models their faces, and so on? That's because those are their biggest assets!

It's activity time, so put on your thinking cap.

1. Comparing Health Insurance Options

Insurance Type	Pros	Cons	Price
Parents' Insurance			
Medicaid			
COBRA			
Employer Plan			
Short term Policy			

Subsidized State Program			
Individual Policy			
Health Insurance Marketplace			

2. Comparing Health Insurance plans

Look up a few health insurance plans online, or talk to them over the phone. Choose any 5 insurance companies, and compare their plans.

Insurer	Type of Plan	Coverage	Cost

 # 3. Find out what type of car insurance is mandatory in your state, and if you plan to drive through or to another state, the type of car insurance that is mandatory there, and the minimum insurance you need to purchase.

State	Mandatory Insurance	Minimum Amount

#4. Just as you compared health insurance plans, compare car insurance plans from five different companies.

Insurer	Type of Plan	Coverage	Cost

I think that you've got the hang of insurance by now. What say we move forward, and proceed to the next station in this journey of financial literacy?

☆☆☆

Part 4

Long-term Financial Success

We have now come to the last part of our book – Financial Endurance, or Long-term Success. What do we mean by that? Endurance means being able to do something for an extended period. Ergo, financial endurance means, maintaining good finances or continuing to be financially successful in the long run.

Let's see a couple of examples of teenagers who started making big money as teenagers and continued to stay rich their whole lives.

Oprah Winfrey

Who doesn't know Oprah? The queen of talk shows got her first job in the media at age 16, as a broadcaster for WVOL, a radio station in Nashville. When she was 19 and in her sophomore year at Tennessee State University, she got an offer from a local TV station. She took a gamble, leaving school to get started on her career. And what a gamble it turned out to be!

Oprah is a household name today – over five decades of success. She is worth a whopping 3 billion US dollars currently.

Elon Musk

Having bought his first computer at the age of 10, Elon Musk wrote code for a video game called Blastar when he was 12. A year later a software engineer at Google transformed the code and developed the game – Musk had made his first $$$. He studied in some of the best schools around the world before joining the Wharton School of Business.

Now, he owns several companies like Tesla and SpaceX and is the world's richest man as of now. His net worth today – a humungous 304 billion US Dollars.

Here are some common traits these successful teens had or developed:

- They started earning early
- They learned skills that would build value
- They saved a portion of every single paycheck
- They avoided or minimized debt, including student debt.
- They sought real-world experience regardless of the wage by prioritizing experience
- They invested in themselves
- They avoided frivolous expenses
- They allowed their money to grow – that part of their money that they invested, they didn't touch.
- They put their money to work and took advantage of the power of compounding

If you see, these are all things that we've been discussing in our book, aren't they? Do you know something else these two, and others like Bill Gates, Mark Zuckerberg, and Richard Branson didn't cave into? Peer pressure. It may seem like it's nothing, but it is huge.

Let's dive straight into what peer pressure is and how to withstand it; we will also discuss how to resist the urge for impulse buying.

★★★

Chapter 8

Combating Peer Pressure and Impulse Buying

Peer Pressure and its Pitfalls

What exactly is peer pressure?

Peers are your classmates, or kids who are in the same activities as you, say, for example, your teammates in football.

All your peers need not be your friends, but all your friends are definitely your peers. The pressure these guys can put on you to do certain things or to act a certain way is what is called peer pressure.

Peer pressure can be about dressing, social behavior, drinking alcohol, smoking, drugs, physical relationships – a lot of things; there is also a lot of financial peer pressure.

Though this can start at school itself, it is more pronounced in college. That's because you are surrounded by your peers, and usually, you don't have any adults around to tell you what's right.

According to *The Guardian,* a mind-boggling **44% of youngsters aged 16 to 24 responded that they are pressured by their peers** to dish out money even when they are scraping the barrel.

Mind you, this influence or pressure doesn't work that much once they cross that age, with only 23% of 25- to 34-year-olds giving in to peer pressure to spend.

You, my friend, are either already in that age group or fast approaching it, and you are the most vulnerable to peer pressure.

Let's look at some real-life examples of peer pressure:

1. Katie, 15, was going to a party with her friends, and it was the first time she was going to a party where older boys would be there – and it had no adults. Though she had never even had wine before, her friends pressured her into doing tequila shots because, well, everyone was doing it, and they would look like ninnies if they didn't. Katie ended up with alcohol poisoning and spent a couple of days in the hospital.
2. Rory, 17, came from a blue-collar family; as a brilliant student, he got a full scholarship to a top law school. His peers were mostly from wealthy families and ridiculed his hand-me-downs. Determined to keep up with them, he splurged his money on branded shirts and sneakers, running into debt that his parents could not afford to pay off.
3. Brad, 16, was talked into boosting cars by his friends; though he was against it at first, he caved under the pressure and found it exciting. He got caught by the cops and had to face the embarrassment of being thrown out of his school.

Of course, it's not always negative; there can be some positive influences as well, which can push you to do your best.

For example, if you happen to be part of a very decent and sober bunch of your peers, they could influence you to, say, be more environmentally conscious, stay away from drugs, or even study harder for tests. That kind of peer pressure can actually be very good for you.

Unfortunately, though, most peer pressure is negative and causes kids to do stuff that can have bad consequences for them, as we saw above.

Why do teens and young adults give in to peer pressure?

It's because as human beings, we all want to fit in; we fear being rejected and isolated. We don't want to stand out and march to the beat of a different drummer. We want to lose ourselves in a crowd. At that age, this desire to blend in with the crowd and be a faceless entity is at its highest.

You don't want to draw attention to yourself; you worry about being bullied, ridiculed, and called out. And it's totally understandable. I feel you; because, once, I WAS you. I too caved in; I too wanted to fit in; I too wanted to blend in and disappear – often with disastrous results.

Now we come to the question: How do we resist this peer pressure?

You need to be strong and confident in yourself, your abilities, and your qualities, in order to resist peer pressure. But I know, it's easier said than done; not everyone is made that way. However, here are some tips to help you:

- Be aware of the reality of peer pressure and plan ahead. Think: How are you going to respond in a particular situation? Have a few ideas of what you will say or do.
- It helps to stay in touch with your parents or guardians. Talk to them daily, or at least a couple of times a week. They are people who have your best interests at heart. It's good for them to know who your friends and classmates

are, and they will be able to make better judgment calls. Set up some kind of code with them – so that when you use those words over a call or on a text, they know that you are in a bad situation, and can come to get you out. Of course, this won't work if they are in another city.

- If your parents live very far away, confide in a counselor or teacher, someone who is trustworthy and will do the right thing for you, and get you out of difficult situations.
- What does your gut say? If you feel something's not right, it probably isn't. Trust your instincts. Don't be part of a situation that you're not okay with, even if your friends are. Walk away.
- Tell those who are suggesting a frivolous or expensive purchase that you need time to think about it and cannot make a decision right away.
- Tell your peer or peers who are putting pressure on you that you are clearly uncomfortable with what they are suggesting, and that you are NOT interested in going forward with it. Request them to stop, politely; if they don't listen to you, repeat your request firmly, and maybe a little forcefully.
- Give an excuse to not go along with what your friends are suggesting; it could be that they want to eat out at a fancy restaurant, and you know it's going to cost a lot. Ideally, you should be able to say "no" without having to apologize or explain yourself, but you could give an excuse to keep the peace; like maybe say you have an allergy to something they serve, or that you have a stomach flu, or some such thing. Or that you have an important test coming up and have to study for it.
- Give them an alternative idea – that will give them something to think about, and buy you time, too.
- You can always be truthful and tell them that you can't afford it.

- Be friends with kids who share the values and beliefs that you have; this will greatly reduce the possibility of unwanted peer pressure. That is more important than being in the 'cool kids' circle. Believe me, being in a group where you have nothing in common with others but are desperate to be part of to be popular, will only give you grief, in more ways than one.
- Tell yourself that it's okay to be the odd one out sometimes, and that you don't have to fit in all the time. Remember, those who conquered nations, built nations, and became famous all over the world, did not do it by fitting in; they did it by standing out. Dare to be different; dare to do the right thing.

So you see, there are ways that you can try to resist peer pressure. Of course, it is possible that the very first time you encounter such a situation, you may not succeed, but you can eventually get it right if you keep at it.

Impulse Buying and its Consequences

We all know what impulse buying is, right? We see something and we fall in love with it, and we want to get our hands on it right away; no matter the price tag, we buy it. And that is a dangerous thing. Dangerous, because it can burn a hole in your pocket all the way from Alaska to Hawaii.

The reasons for impulse buying are pretty similar to buying because of peer pressure; well, at least most of the time. It's because your peers have those things that you also feel like buying. The pressure is internal. At times, it happens even if you don't see anyone else with a similar cool jacket or backpack. It just looks so amazing that you absolutely MUST have it. Feel familiar? Or, it's at 70% off, and it's a great steal deal. It's a never before, and probably never later offer, so better buy it.

Ah yes, we've all had those feelings at some point in life.

I. The Psychology of Impulse Buying

Let's take a look at the triggers or psychology behind impulse purchases:

1. Emotions

Emotions can drive behavior like nothing else can, and marketers use this very smartly. Ads are one of the ways they do it – using beautiful visuals and music that influence your mind to buy something right away. Have you noticed how they play music in supermarkets and apparel stores? Ah well, that's because music has the power to improve your mood. You feel happy and are more likely to buy something you see.

2. Social Influence

This is what we talked about before – indirect peer pressure. You buy something to fit in with the "cool" crowd.

3. Cognitive Biases

Cognitive biases are often caused by imbibing only the initial or part of the information about a product and then base their decision to purchase on that information.

Clever marketers take advantage of this bias by pricing those products higher. When people don't make informed decisions, they often end up with wrong purchases.

You know what they say – haste makes waste!

This is also called the need for instant gratification – after all, we live in such a world. We have replaced our books with videos, movies with reels... the shorter, the better.

Text messages use minimal alphabets. We have no time and no patience to wait for the good things anymore.

II. Cost vs. Value

It is important here to know the difference and correlation between cost and value.

Just because something has a high price tag does not mean that it is good in quality or something that is useful. Similarly, just because something is cheap does not mean it's a good deal. You have to find the balance between price and value.

A product must be cost-effective. That's not the same as being cheap. For example, buying a $80 pair of sneakers is quite likely to be much better than buying a $30 pair of sneakers, because, in all likelihood, the cheap sneakers may give out in just a couple of weeks.

Quality also matters. You don't need to go for the best brand or the most expensive, but it's got to be decent, right? The cost of the second pair is lower, sure, but its value is way too low to justify its purchase. You may ask, what is value? Value is the use that you get out of a product or service.

Now what is interesting is that while we can measure value in monetary terms, it can differ from person to person, even for the product costing the same amount.

For example, you may value your second-hand car much more than someone who has two or three new cars. Also, you may value a product less as time goes by. The longer you have your car, the less you may value it, and feel like replacing it with a new one. Fair enough?

To put it in very simple words, you need to truly feel, even after some time, that the purchase was worth it. Not feel, "Oh, no! What have I done? Why on Earth did I buy that?"

A cost-effective product is not necessarily the cheapest or probably even very cheap, but certainly not way too expensive, and that delivers good value to the buyer – in this case, you. Let's go back to the sneaker example.

Let's say you buy a pair for $110. They are comfortable, look good on your feet, and don't get spoiled for a couple of years. I would say they are definitely cost-effective!

III. Delayed Gratification

I just spoke to you about instant gratification being one of the biggest culprits behind impulse purchases. And guess what, marketers gleefully take advantage of this desire of yours to sell their products, and sell them at a high price. So how can delayed gratification help? Let's understand this by learning about the **Marshmallow Experiment.**

This was an experiment conducted by Stanford University in 1971-72. The researchers placed several children in individual rooms with a marshmallow on a table in front of their chairs. Each child was told that if they waited to eat it until the person returned, they would get a second marshmallow. However, if they ate it, that would be the only one they would get to eat.

The result was interesting…

Most children jumped up and ate their marshmallows as soon as the researcher left the room; some kids tried their best to control themselves, squirming and wriggling in their seats, but eventually gave in, and gobbled it up.

There were, however, a few who did manage to NOT eat their marshmallows till the researcher returned. They did get their second treat.

Now, though the report was published in 1972, it didn't end there. These children were tracked for years, as the researchers followed up. They learned that the children who waited the entire 15 minutes were by and large more successful academically, socially, and financially. They made healthier food choices and responded better to stress, peer pressure, and other difficult situations.

Delayed gratification is about discipline; waiting for some time, delaying that instant happiness for a potentially larger reward a little later. In other words, you choose the pain of discipline over the ease of distraction.

Is delayed gratification a trait that can be learned, or is it inborn? Perhaps a bit of both? To find the answers to these questions, the University of Rochester repeated the marshmallow test – with a secret ingredient. They added a twist. The set of children who turned up for the test were split into two groups.

The first group was given reliable experiences. Like, the researchers gave them a set of crayons and coloring books, and were told that they would get better quality crayons and more interesting coloring books later; researchers also gave them stickers and promised better ones later.

After 10-15 minutes of coloring, the kids were given better crayons and books, and more stickers; the researchers kept their promise.

The second group was given unreliable experiences. They were promised the same things as the other kids, but they never got the better crayons and books or stickers. After a while, the children were placed in separate rooms for the marshmallow experiment, and the results were really interesting.

The kids in the first group already had an experience of getting a better item if they waited, so they waited for 15 minutes and only ate the marshmallow when the researchers returned.

The kids in the second group, however, did not believe the adults who told them that waiting would get them a second treat, because it hadn't happened for the first time. They proceeded to eat the marshmallow immediately.

This shows that the brain can be trained to delay gratification. It is possible. It takes practice. Convince your brain that waiting has its rewards, and it's totally worth it.

- One way to do it when you get triggered to buy anything is to tell yourself that you will think about it, and wait for a couple of days to make the final decision. If you're shopping online, there's this wonderful thing you can do called "Add to Cart". You don't have to check out right away! It gives you the satisfaction of having added the item you liked to your cart. Now the website will keep sending you reminders that you've left items in your cart, and urge you to complete the checkout. They don't want you to forget.
- Now here's something interesting: this sometimes has the opposite effect. You find it irritating to be reminded so many times that you simply remove the items from the cart. Of course, if you feel as strongly about the product as you did when you first saw it, then you may want to go ahead and buy it. But usually what happens is that you keep thinking about it, and the more you think critically, the less desirable the product seems to be!

Let's practice what we've learned here:

Activity #1: Get a friend or two, and role play peer pressure and saying no in different ways.

Activity # 2: Make a list of things that you bought on impulse in the past year, and analyze if they were worth it.

____

____

____

____

Now that you have seen how you can keep a lid on your spending, it's time to see how you can build a secure financial future, and how you can continue to generate income without constantly working.

☆☆☆

Chapter 9

Taking Control of Your Financial Future with Passive Income

What is financial freedom? What does it mean to be free financially? At its simplest, it means having enough money for your needs, so that you are not dependent on anyone. It also means that you have sufficient money not just for right now, but also for the immediate or even longer-term future.

Financial freedom is important because it gives you the freedom to live life on your terms, to take up hobbies and activities that you want, travel, study, and even save for your golden years. Having financial freedom means you can do the work you want to do. When you are not financially independent, you cannot choose; you work because you MUST.

A financially independent person can pursue their dreams because their basic needs are well taken care of. One way to do it is the conventional way, what we have been talking about till now. You work, save, invest, repeat. It's a continuous cycle that needs to be followed to ensure you keep generating money.

You take control of your financial future by setting goals. All of these goals may not be directly related to finances, but they are still important.

1. To stay in good health

Why? If you don't, you will waste time and money on hospital/ doctor visits, medicines, procedures, and so on; time and money that could have been used productively instead.

2. **To live below your means**

I can't say this enough; if you have $100, don't spend $110, or even $100. Aim to spend $80, and save or invest the remaining $20.

3. **To plan for your retirement**

We've touched upon this but it's really important; you will get old one day, and the sooner you start putting money away for that eventuality, the more comfortable those days will be.

Don't be shy to talk to a financial advisor; they will help ensure you stay on track to achieve all the goals you set for yourself. They can even conduct a financial health check-up for you maybe once in six months, to see how you're doing.

Here are some important goals you need to have as students; these goals have been defined by actual students who explain why these are critical:

4. **Build an Emergency Fund: Stacey, California Baptist University**

Stacey kept putting money into her emergency fund, even if it meant sacrificing some fun, hip clothes, or cool accessories. And it served her well! She had an accident, and her medical bills ran up to $3,000. Thanks to her emergency fund, she could pay it off without having to ask for help. She made a full recovery and is rebuilding her emergency fund while also doing well academically.

5. **Build your Credit Score – Madison, Notre Dame**

She got her first credit card as a junior and steadily worked at building a credit history by making purchases on the card and paying the bill in full on or before the due date. Her goal? To have a credit score of 800 by the time she graduates, so that she will be eligible for bigger loans or premium cards to help launch her business.

6. **Graduate Debt-free – Alec, University of the Sciences**

Alec wants to make sure that by the time he graduates, he has either paid off his loan in full, or has a very small amount left so he doesn't burden his parents or worry about it when he applies for jobs. By being debt-free, he will be able to choose the job he wants rather than just grab the first thing that comes his way.

7. **Start Budgeting – Alani, Valencia College**

Living alone opened Alani's eyes to some home truths, and she began to notice where exactly her money was going, which she never did back home. She began to set a budget for each month, making sure that she divided every paycheck properly, with a little bit going towards savings. She is determined to live within her means and avoid asking her parents for extra cash.

8. **Earn a Steady Income – Ethan, The Master's University, CA**

Ethan is a business major and plans to follow in his grandfather's and father's footsteps as a realtor. He plans to sell one house each year during his college so that he keeps earning a decent amount without taking much time away from his studies. To support his goal, he is taking real estate lessons.

9. **Generate a Passive Income – Austin, Oklahoma City University**

Austin is one smart cookie, who believes in smart work, not hard work. His goal is to set up a passive income stream that would keep raking in bucks, month after month, year after year, whether he actually worked or not. He has a scholarship, so he is fortunate that he does not have to pay off student loans.

What is Passive Income?

Whoa, whoa, let's take a minute. Passive income – what's that? How do we earn it? And what does Austin mean, making money without working? Is that even possible? To answer you, yes, but not exactly in the way you think.

Let's start at the beginning.

Passive income is income that is generated without putting in the amount of effort you would normally put in at a conventional job. It is something that you set in motion so that it continues to generate income without you needing to keep working at it.

It is probably best understood with a few examples:

- Interest earned from high-yield savings accounts, CDs, ETFs, and other financial instruments
- Rental income earned from renting out your home to tenants.
- Blogs, vlogs, and online content that keep earning you an income once you monetize them
- Books that you write (don't have to be heavy stuff!)

The Interesting Case of Amy Landino: In 2007, with a student loan of $50,000, Amy Landino made the shocking decision to drop out of college. She had a dream, a goal that was achievable. Seventeen years later, she earns (roughly) a jaw-dropping $18,000 a month from her business! How did she do it? She set up streams of passive income. Here's what she has to say, which is great advice for anyone wanting to build a passive income stream:

1. Build one revenue stream at a time:

While it is easy to get carried away and want to expand and scale your business before you have one successful model, don't. Be patient, and don't diversify your revenue in this manner. Amy says that the wise thing to do is to focus on one revenue stream, work out the kinks, and make sure it works before you plunge into the next one.

She worked with a social media marketer and learned the process well enough to design her own course. During her stint at the agency, she learned to:

- Identify what her audience wanted
- Create and market digital products
- Set the right price
- Automate delivery and provide support.

She waited patiently until this system worked, and then turned to other revenue streams – related, of course. Her patience paid off because her next venture had a strong foundation to take off from; a foundation that was built on real-world success.

Amy says don't rush to diversify; rather, take your time to work through the hurdles of building your first revenue stream successfully. There's one thing I would like to mention here; this diversification should not be confused with the investment portfolio diversification that we discussed earlier.

When you're building your first income stream, by all means, make small investments in CDs, bonds, and stocks as well. Those are also passive income streams, but they are in an entirely different investment type.

Coming back to passive income streams, the skills you develop and the lessons you learn, will make you better at creating and growing new ones.

2. Allow your audience to guide your growth:

Now, this is very important; your target audience, your customer base, points you in the direction you should take. This is something followed by all savvy marketers. A good example of this would be changing fashions. When customers start fancying a new style, designers are compelled to follow suit.

Retailers are compelled to stock what the customers want; If you want to sell, you must offer what your customers want. Amy, being an influencer, wrote a book on video content strategy because her followers asked her for it. Similarly, when you set up your passive income stream, find out what your audience wants or cares about, and create your content around it.

Amy's second book also had spin-off ideas for products, like a planner, which was another revenue stream. Merchandise sold by gaming companies is an additional income stream; they already earn from the game.

Basically, your target audience will tell you what they want to buy; it's important that you listen to them, and deliver the goods. Literally.

3. Build systems that keep generating revenue:

Amy says that working just a few hours a day does not mean you work less; it just means that you work smart! You don't need an 8-hour workday to create a video or even a couple of reels. In 3-4 hours of work a day, you can create content that continues to earn long after it is up on the web.

Amy has made over a thousand videos about building your brand, increasing productivity, and so on. Sure, it sounds huge when you say it like that, but she has simply been consistent and systematic, continuing to create content steadily. Every piece of content she created does its part in generating passive income.

With the right content, one that delivers value to your audience, you can build a powerful income-generating engine that serves you for years.

4. Continue to Learn:

Amy did not stop learning just because she dropped out of college. She kept adding to her armory, the skills she needed to be numero uno at her work, like writing books, editing videos, developing products, and more. She also had to learn to stay motivated and keep going, facing her challenges head-on.

Here's a critical lesson for you. Challenges will come; hurdles will appear; you may fall; however, you must continue to work towards your goal. Giving up is not an option. A little child, a toddler, when he or she starts walking, often falls several times. Do they give up? No, they keep getting up and try again and again, till they are steady on their feet.

You did it too, as a toddler. So, you can do it too. Learn through trial and error. Mistakes should not stop you from achieving your goals. Invest in courses and mentors if needed, and get better at what you do.

The reason I chose to speak at length about Amy is that she has some solid lessons to give us in terms of building passive income streams, and about life itself. And it comes from her own experience – so it is believable.

<u>The Best Passive Income Streams for Teens and Young Adults:</u>

- Renting out your spare room
- Investing in high-yield savings accounts, bonds, stocks
- Automating your savings and investments; set up auto transfers from your savings account to specific investments or savings accounts each month.
- Renting out your car
- Creating content – blogs or vlogs
- Write ebooks
- Selling digital products
- Affiliate marketing
- Buying and selling websites/domains
- Sell your photos and designs online
- Rent out photography equipment (if you have any)

- Create and sell courses
- Print-on-demand stores
- Get paid for downloading apps or shopping
- Watch videos for money
- Get paid to use less electricity
- Get paid to stay fit with apps like Oppizi, Diet Bet, Sweat Coin, etc.
- Invest in sports cards

Let's do a recap of the benefits of earning passive income:

- Turn your hobby into your income
- It offers financial freedom and stability
- Achieve financial goals quicker
- Freedom from paycheck dependency
- You get the flexibility to live life on your terms
- Enables you to pursue your dreams
- Ability to indulge in your favorite activities
- Reduces stress and frees up your time
- Accumulate wealth
- Retire early

Here is one thing I would like to bring to your notice: when we say passive income, we don't mean that you build one thing, or say, two things, and then you can stop working. No. You must keep working, building more streams of passive income, so that each stream continues to generate income in the long term. Let's say one of the streams peters out because that subject is no longer popular – when you have other streams of income, it won't create a dent in your earnings.

For example, let's say that you created a course on how to develop your negative films into photos, a few years ago. With the advent of digital photography, slowly, the buyers for this course would have reduced and eventually stopped. But if you have created other courses or content, then you will have nothing to worry about.

You have to nurture your passive income stream, but it takes a lot less work than working a 9 to 5-job. Many people do both – work part-time at a conventional job, because it offers some sort of security, and also creates passive income streams. Some people work full-time, and create digital content on the weekends and on holidays.

You can also try this method. Once your passive income stream establishes and takes off, bringing you solid income, you can slowly transition to it full-time. Remember, smart work, not hard!

Passive income is the best way for you to have plenty of free time, while still doing work that you love.

Let's do an activity that will help you understand it even better!

#Make a list of possible passive income streams depending on your skills and interests; work out how much you will need to spend on setting it up, and the potential income you can earn from it.

Passive Income Idea	Cost of setup	Potential income	Estimated timeframe

Great! You are now all set; armed with the knowledge of how to earn money through a number of methods across diverse fields. How to plan for your financial freedom, your retirement, your needs, and your happiness.

Once you've achieved all of this, there is something very important that you need to think about, and that, my friend, is giving back. That's where we will focus on the next and last chapter of our book. The ultimate destination of this exciting, educational, and fun journey that we've been having.

★★★

Chapter 10

The Power of Philanthropy

Here we are – having navigated all the ways of making and saving money, it is now time to help others; those who are less fortunate than us; those who haven't been able to make it in life for various reasons – circumstances, disabilities, illnesses, lack of education or awareness, or anything else.

Let's Explore Charitable Giving

Communities everywhere face several problems; life is hard. Some are homeless, many don't have enough food, many don't have proper access to healthcare. Many animals need care and protection.

Now you may think that it's the government's job to provide for such people, not mine. Well, the government does have funds for such activities, but it is not nearly enough. That is why you and I, and others like us, need to step in. We have within us, the power to bring positive change where it is needed the most.

There are many ways in which you can help others and many different causes that you can support. We will explore all this and more in this chapter.

How You Can Make a Difference

There's a saying that love makes the world go 'round, and it is absolutely true. When you do philanthropy, you bring benefits to people, society, our communities, and the planet as a whole.

When you start paying it forward, when you share what you have with those who genuinely need it, that is when you become mature – no matter what your age may be. Philanthropy is a powerful tool that can cause long-term social change. When you support a nonprofit organization, there's a domino effect, as you can potentially touch many lives.

In fact, philanthropy is thought to be one of the main pillars of a stable and thriving society. Whenever you join hands with others to donate your time or money, you get a real sense of what it means to be a human being. You can help your community grow stronger.

Philanthropy is defined as "the genuine desire to ensure the welfare of others, usually by generously donating money to good causes." However, philanthropy is much more than that. It has numerous positive effects on the world.

Way back in 1630, John from Massachusetts Bay Colony told the Puritan settlers that those who are wealthy must care for those who are not; those who could not help themselves should be helped by others. 8 years later, John Harvard left half of his estate to start Harvard University – one of the most famous universities in the world.

Check out these stats:

According to the Indiana University Lilly Family School of Philanthropy annual report, in 2023, Americans, big business corporations, and other organizations together donated a total of over 557 billion US dollars to charities nationwide. The annual report of Giving USA tells us that:

- **Individuals donated over 374 billion USD**
- **Foundations donated more than 103 billion USD**
- **Corporations donated over 36 billion USD**
- **Over 42 billion USD came via trusts and wills** – it was bequeathed by individuals

I hope this gives you a good idea of how seriously people take philanthropy. Just imagine what can be achieved with such a huge amount! In a world of Scrooges, it's these angels who keep the world going, giving hope to billions of people to carry on.

And don't think for a moment, I'll start giving to charity when I become an adult and have a steady job and whatnot. That day will never come. Believe me, the earlier you start, the better. Let's rewind a bit, and go back to the very first chapter, where we spoke about Ryan Hreljac. You remember him, right?

He was just 7 when he heard how children in Africa were dying because they didn't have clean water to drink. From that day, he decided he would build wells for them. Such a little soul, such a huge dream. He didn't have any money, so he did whatever jobs he could to make the money for the well.

If such a little boy could understand the need to help others, well, I'm sure that as a teenager, you definitely can!

There are many different forms of philanthropy or charitable giving. It can be an ongoing donation, a one-time donation, it could even be through using your time and effort to help; how is that charity? Well, if you had used that time to work and earn, you would have money in your pocket. But you chose to forego that money and help people instead, so yes, it counts as charity.

The Benefits of Doing Charity

Why do people do charity? Why should you? There are many benefits of philanthropy, let's discuss a few common ones.

1. Emotional reasons:

Many non-profit organizations are doing incredible work to provide help to the needy – both people and animals. Almost all of us are bound to be attracted to a particular cause because we feel some kind of emotional connection with it. If you love animals deeply, you may feel inclined to help an animal shelter or welfare organization. Or perhaps you feel very deeply for children and want to help children who are victims of abuse, and so on.

2. You can make a difference:

When you make a donation or volunteer your time and/or effort, regardless of the size of your donation or the length of time; regardless of how big, small, or widespread that nonprofit is, you are making a REAL difference. It is because of the generosity of individuals like you that these charities are able to carry on their good work. Ergo, your decision to donate to a charitable organization makes a real impact on the lives of the people (or animals) that charity helps.

3. Every little donation helps:

Whether you donate a larger amount one time, or small donations every month or year, your contribution matters, and it helps. Every donation the charity receives adds up and makes a difference. Don't worry that you don't have a great deal to spare, just focus on what you can. The organization/individual you help will be grateful for it.

4. Charity reaches the most vulnerable section of our communities:

Quite often, those who need help the most get overlooked; the government is not equipped to protect and provide for everyone in need. This is where charitable organizations and individuals step in and do what's needed. This could be to help seniors who are all alone, homeless people, abused children, abandoned animals, and so on. Your contributions in cash and kind help everyone – like the Marines say, no man left behind!

5. Gives us a sense of belonging:

Helping to reduce hardships for others, and remembering that we are all in it together, helps us feel more connected with those around us, and be an active part of our community.

6. Set an example for others:

Everyone is capable of making a difference; so, you can inspire others to do their bit and boost the impact of charity. When friends, family, classmates, and neighbors see what you're doing, I bet you, they will be motivated to pitch in as well.

7. Giving is in our nature:

Human beings have a protective instinct, and history tells us that societies flourished because people stuck together, helped each other, and worked together. Being selfless allows us to provide for those who need it the most.

8. It makes us feel good:

Now this is a fact. When you do good deeds, you definitely deserve a pat on your back. You feel good about yourself, and that puts you in a good mood. It makes you productive, helps you focus, and be better at your studies, work, or sports.

9. Enjoy a little tax relief:

Charitable donations can help you bring down your taxable income – if you are a taxpayer because your income is above a certain level, being philanthropic will help you save a little on your tax.

How Can you Donate your Time?

As a teenager or young adult, here are some ways you can donate your time:

- Volunteer at soup kitchens to serve food
- Volunteer at homeless shelters to clean, do laundry, etc.
- Read to older people living in a senior facility, or even in your neighborhood, and run chores for them like picking up their laundry, walking their pets, helping them understand and use digital products and new technology, and so on. Sometimes they just need someone to talk to – old people are often lonely. Spend some time with them, chat with them, maybe make them a cup of tea, and they will bless you for it. You can also help them with decorating their homes for Halloween, Christmas, and other festivals.
- Care for animals in a shelter by feeding them, cleaning them, and taking them for walks or vet appointments.
- Participate in your school's learning-based charity programs
- Get involved in service projects at your church, temple, mosque, etc.
- Participate in community service programs.
- Give free tuition, teach music or art, teach cleanliness, etc. to homeless children or those in shelters.

- Join the Red Cross
- Babysit children in your neighborhood or community for free; offer this service only to those who are struggling financially.
- Volunteer for a crisis hotline like TeenLineOnline.org
- Help specially-abled children at school and in your community with daily chores or studies
- Volunteer at county hospitals to make the healthcare experience better for patients
- Teach English to immigrant children and adults
- Collect used clothes, books, and toys from your neighborhood to donate to children's hospitals and shelters; ensure that they are in good condition.

How Can you Donate Money or Raise Funds?

If you have a job, even a part-time one, make it a point to set aside a small portion of your paycheck for charity. You can collect it for a few months, or weeks, depending on how much you can afford to set aside, and go and then donate it to a charity that you care about.

You can also set up fundraisers. Many people ask their friends and family to donate to their chosen charity instead of buying them birthday presents, and that's such an amazing thing to do, don't you think? There are many ways that you can organize fundraisers:

- Host a bake sale in your community
- Sell lemonade
- Sell raffle tickets and hold a lucky draw, giving away a small prize, with the rest of the proceeds going to charity.
- Sell candy, cookies, or other home-baked goodies door-to-door or at community centers.
- Sell handmade art or crafts.

- Make use of brands like Little Caesars® Pizza Kit Fundraising Program, See's Candy Fundraising, and so on. They have different options like pre-sold orders, drop shipping, bulk selling (by the carton), and more. The What a Crock Fundraising program delivers home-cooked meals to your supporters, and you get to keep 20% of the profits for your favorite charity.
- Host a virtual event—such as a gaming competition, where players have to pay a fee to participate. Offer a small prize to the winner and donate the rest.
- Hold a garage sale where you sell old things that you no longer need. You could even collect items from schoolmates and neighbors.
- Crowd funding is a very popular method of fundraising today. You simply spread the word about a cause, and request donations from people, either in cash or in kind.
- Start a Go Fund Me account, with your guardian as the beneficiary, as only an adult is allowed to withdraw funds; ask people to donate money to your account.
- Conduct a mini-marathon or run for a specific cause and set up peer-to-peer fundraising to encourage donations.
- Organize a mini carnival, with fun games held either in your school, home, or community center; check what permissions you will need to do this. Each game can be charged; give away token prizes, and donate your collections to your cause.
- Conduct a dance-off competition, a singing competition, or even a painting competition. Charge a participation fee, and sell tickets to the show.
- Partner with a local farm and create a pumpkin patch event, charging an entry fee, or requesting donations for pumpkins and photographs.

The thing to remember in all of these ideas is that you need to offer the participants something – it doesn't have to be expensive;

it can be a token gift or prize, but give them something so that they enjoy the event.

Use social media to the fullest extent possible to publicize your fundraising event, whether it is offline or online. Make sure that you grab the attention of as many people as you can. Use Instagram, X, Facebook, Threads, TikTok, Pinterest, and even SMSes to let people know about your event.

Take someone's help – a parent or guardian would be ideal, especially to manage the money part. If not, form a small group with your friends, and divvy up the chores and tasks, so that you are not overwhelmed.

Most Importantly, Be SCRUPULOUSLY honest. Not even a single dollar should be unaccounted for. Everything that you receive and everything that you spend, must be recorded without fail, and properly. Anyone should be able to look at your accounts and instantly know where the money came from, where it went, and so on. I can't say this enough! After all, you want people to trust you, so you must make sure that you are trustworthy.

I would like to conclude with the example of Mychal-Bella Bowman, a Hollywood child star. At the tender age of 12, she has already won an Emmy and Golden Globe for her role as Grace in the "The Underground Railroad". She has also modeled from the time she was a toddler, for Barbie, Nike, and GAP, and appeared in ads for Disney, Target, McDonald's, and Hertz, among others.

She always had a kind heart, donating her gently used toys to poor kids as a little child. Today, she works with nonprofits, helping them to spread awareness about bullying and mental health, assist the homeless, and support children's education.

So, my friend, it's never too early to start giving! We have seen two big examples of children who started charitable activities at a young age; I'm pretty sure there are plenty more out there. You can do it too, you just need to put your mind to it.

Activity

Make a list of causes that you feel strongly about, and write down how much a month you will be able to donate toward it.

And with that, we've reached the end of our journey together. It has been an amazing experience, and I hope that you've not only enjoyed reading it as much as I enjoyed writing it; I truly hope that you have some positive takeaways from 'Cash Me If You Can'.

Final Thoughts

What a rollercoaster of a ride we were on and I am so glad you were a part of this journey with me.

Now comes the question:

Can we say that we are financially literate after this?

I'd say there's always a lot more to learn, but this will give you an idea of what is out there in terms of understanding finance.

'Cash Me If You Can' began with the promise of helping you learn to be financially independent. We first explored what financial literacy is and why it is important. Statistics tell us that even today, far too many people are not financially literate, and this leads to all kinds of problems.

People make poor choices, most often because they don't know any better. Growing up, I too didn't have a guardian angel advising me what to do with my money. And that's what I have tried to do here – to guide you to be responsible with money.

We saw how even teens and young adults like you can not just manage the money they get from parents or guardians properly but also how you can earn adequate money for your own needs, to start with. You can work your way up to earning better so that you can lead a comfortable life and retire early. After all, that is what most of us want in the end, right?

We also discussed how with just a little hard work and some smart choices, we can pursue our dreams – go on holidays, buy the car we wanted, or anything else.

The various ways in which you can make money, the different jobs you could do – we went through it all.

We saw how we could make budgets, mark money for each expense, and make sure to keep some aside to save up for emergencies. Budgeting apps and tools, distinguishing between needs and wants, building an emergency fund, and all of that stuff is important.

Making the right and good choices is hard, yes; but it is definitely worth it in the end. Saving and investing were the next thing we learned, and it must have come as a surprise to you that even you could invest. I hope you will start making some money with part-time jobs, and take your parent's help to save and invest.

We also saw countless real-life examples of people who began earning at an early age, and how they built a good life and continued with it throughout their lives. We also saw people who threw it all away by making poor choices.

The importance of self-control cannot be stressed enough. If I've said it a million times already, I'll say it one more time. You need to be a little disciplined and make a few sacrifices.

You now know all about the kind of insurance that is important for you, how you can get it, what the different types of insurance are, and so on.

I hope that you will not just be smart with managing your money now, but also savvy enough to not fall for scammers. Always remember – if something sounds too good to be true, it probably is!

It would be great if you seriously set about building your first stream of passive income right away. It shouldn't be a problem – your generation is already great at making videos, reels, and whatnot! There are even a lot of simple business ideas in there.

Finally, we discussed why it is important to give back; it is good for your soul, and good for society. If you can't give money, donate your time. Sometimes, that is appreciated a lot more than a financial contribution.

Being in command of your future is so much easier when you are financially independent; and being financially independent can happen only with the right guidance, practice, and determination to keep doing the right thing.

Here's a suggestion from me: to know the true value of money, of every single dollar, start with an ordinary job – waiting tables, flipping burgers, bagging groceries, washing cars – or anything like that. When you make small money, you start appreciating and valuing it. When the $$$ becomes big money you will be wise to not waste but be smart.

Once you work for some time at small jobs like these, you can slowly move on to more serious jobs, like working in a proper office. There too, maybe you can think of interning first. Starting from the lower rung always gives you a better sense of the place you're working in.

I strongly recommend that you take the worksheets and activities seriously, and work them out; put on your thinking cap, and you will become adept at actually using those skills in real life.

Earning, saving, and managing your money well, investing it, and making it grow, will all become habits, and just like driving or swimming, you will do them automatically.

Well, so this is the end of the road. But hey, there's no permanent goodbye! You are welcome to stay in touch with me and reach out to me via email (domajithsingh@gmail.com) should you need any clarification of your queries, or guidance on any specific subject.

I promise to do the best I can to help you. This is one of the ways that I am giving back. I wish you the very best in life and do hope that you achieve everything that you have always wanted.

God Bless!

★★★